A CHILD'S BIBLE

Lessons from the Prophets and Writings

Seymour Rossel

BEHRMAN HOUSE

A CHILD'S BIBLE

Lessons from the Prophets and Writings

Seymour Rossel

BEHRMAN HOUSE

Dedicated to my brother and my friend
CARY ROSSEL
As it is written, "Jonathan's soul was
bound up with the soul of David; for Jonathan
loved David as himself" [I Samuel 18:1].
S.R.

PROJECT EDITOR: RUBY G. STRAUSS

BOOK DESIGN: ROBERT J. O'DELL

ILLUSTRATIONS: JOHN SANDFORD

PHOTO CREDITS

11 (lower) Chuck Muhlstock/Black Star; **26** (upper) FourByFive; **50** (upper) United Federation of MetroWest; **67** (lower) Cantor Mordecai M. Goldstein; **94** (lower) FourByFive; **129** (lower) Eve Arnold/Magnum; **130** United Federation of MetroWest; **156** (upper) Benjamin Joseph Cutter; **157** (lower) Rich Russo Photography.

Through special arrangement with The Jerusalem Publishing House Ltd.: **11** (upper), **12**, **17-19**, **27**, **33-34**, **41-42**, **50** (lower), **51**, **58-59**, **67** (upper), **68**, **77-78**, **86-87**, **93**, **94** (upper), **103-104**, **111-113**, **120-121**, **129** (upper), **139-140**, **148-149**, **157** (upper).

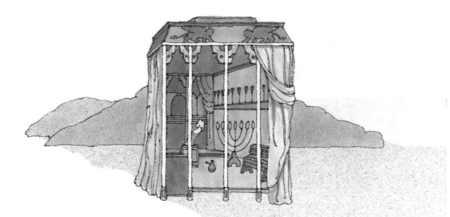

PUBLISHED BY BEHRMAN HOUSE, INC.
235 Watchung Avenue, West Orange, New Jersey 07052
ISBN 0-87441-487-3

MANUFACTURED IN THE UNITED STATES OF AMERICA

CONTENTS

6

So it shall be in time to come:
When your child asks you, "What is this?"
you shall say, "God's own strength
brought us out of Egypt, out of the house
of slavery." [Exodus 13:14]

D U C T I O N

The Bible is the history of the covenant between God and our people. It begins with the Five Books of Moses, the Torah.

The Torah tells how God created the world and rested on the Seventh day. You meet Adam and Eve in the Garden of Eden, and learn the sad tale of their children, Cain and Abel. You hear about Noah and the ark and how God made a covenant with Noah, leaving the rainbow as a sign that the world would never again be destroyed by flood.

In the Torah you find God's promise to Abraham, to make the children of Abraham and Sarah into a great nation with a land of their own. You read the stories of Abraham and Sarah; of Isaac and Rebecca; and of Rachel, Leah, and Jacob. You see Joseph sold into slavery by his brothers and learn how Joseph put his faith in God and became a ruler in Egypt, second only to Pharaoh himself.

In the Torah you see how Pharaoh welcomed the Children of Israel into Egypt, where our people grew many in number, just as God promised. You learn about a new Pharaoh who did not remember the good that Joseph did for Egypt. You feel the years of pain when our people were forced to serve Pharaoh as slaves. Until, at last, the pain was too much to bear, and God heard the cries of the Hebrew slaves and sent Moses to Egypt to tell Pharaoh, "Let My people go!"

These things are the history of our people, your history. The Bible reminds you that you are not alone in this world. You are a part of the people of Israel, the Jewish people that promised to be God's people. The Bible – the Torah, the Prophets, and the Writings – is your history as a Jew.

As this book begins, the Children of Israel are following Moses, the greatest of our Prophets. They are not slaves any more. They are beginning the long journey to the land that God promised to Abraham. The land is not far away, but the people are not yet ready for it. They grew up as slaves and, in many ways, they still behave like slaves. Before the land can be theirs, they must learn new lessons. You will be with them as they discover what it means to be free, what is means to be a people in its own land, and what it means to walk in God's ways.

Chapter 1

CROSSING THE SEA OF REEDS

 t came to pass—when Pharaoh let the Children of Israel go—that God led the people the wilderness way to the Sea of Reeds. By day, God went before them like a great cloud showing the way, and by night the cloud turned to fire giving them light. So they marched by day and by night. And God was always before them.

God said to Moses: "Tell the Children of Israel to camp by the sea. I will make Pharaoh and all his army come after them. And I will defeat Pharaoh and all his army. Then the Egyptians will know that I am God."

Then Pharaoh thought, "Why have we let Israel go? Who will be our slaves now that they are gone?" So Pharaoh gathered his army of six hundred horses and chariots to chase after the Children of Israel. They caught up with the Israelites as they camped on the shore of the sea.

Suddenly the Children of Israel lifted their eyes and saw the Egyptians coming toward them. They were greatly afraid, and their cries reached to the heavens. They complained to Moses, "Why have you taken us to the wilderness? We would rather be slaves in Egypt than die in the wilderness."

Moses spoke gently to the people. "Do not be afraid. See how God will save you. The Egyptians you see today, you shall see again no more forever."

And God said to Moses, "Tell the Children of Israel to go forward. Just lift up your rod, and stretch your hand over the sea." Then the great cloud went behind the Children of Israel, so that the Egyptians did not come near the Israelites all that night.

Moses stretched out his hand over the sea. God lashed the sea with a strong east wind, dividing the waters, and making the sea into dry land. The Children of Israel crossed the sea on dry ground, and the waters of the sea were a wall on their right and a wall on their left.

The Egyptians chased after them. They drove between the walls of water – all Pharaoh's horses, his mighty chariots, and his horsemen. In the morning, God looked down upon the army of the Egyptians through the fire and cloud, and God trapped the chariots. The earth turned to mud and the wheels of the chariots were caught. The Egyptians said, "Let us flee, for God fights for the Israelites against the Egyptians."

Then God said to Moses, "Stretch out your hand over the sea, that the waters may close upon the Egyptians." And Moses stretched out his hand over the sea. Then the waters rushed in, covering the chariots, drowning the horsemen, and closing over all the army of Pharaoh. Not even one of them remained. So God saved Israel that day.

When Israel saw the great work which God had done, the people feared God, and believed in God and Moses. Then Miriam the prophetess, the sister of Moses and Aaron, took her hand drum. All the women danced with her. And all Israel sang this song:

> I will sing to God,
>> For God's great victory!
> The horse and its rider
>> God has thrown into the sea!

> Who is like You, O God, among the gods?
>> Who is like You,
> Glorious in holiness,
>> Colossal in praises,
> Doing wonders?

Then Moses led the Children of Israel away from the Sea of Reeds, into the wilderness, toward the land of Canaan.

This picture of Pharaoh in his chariot leading his armies is painted on the side of a chest.

WHAT DOES IT MEAN?

God led the people the wilderness way...

The Israelites did not have to go through the wilderness. There was a much shorter way from Egypt to Canaan, a way which would take no more than ten or twelve days! Instead God chose to lead the people through the wilderness, a journey which lasted forty years!

The short way led through the land of the Philistines. These warriors would not have let a people like the Israelites pass without a fight. True, the Israelites had weapons with them. But God said, "The people might change their minds if they see war. They might return to Egypt."

The short way of doing things is not always the best way. *Learning new things takes time.* It would take the Children of Israel nearly forty years to learn the true meaning of freedom. For the moment they knew more about being slaves. As they said to Moses, "We would rather be slaves in Egypt than die in the wilderness." Forty years later, the people would never say such a thing. The value of freedom, especially the freedom to worship God, is one of the great lessons of the Bible.

A gymnast performing on the high bar. It takes day-by-day practice to do well—in sports or in life.

The Wind and the Manna

The Torah tells of many miracles. In the wilderness, the Israelites found themselves without food. They complained to Moses, "Oh, that we had died in the land of Egypt, where we sat by pots of meat and ate all the bread we wanted! For you have brought us out into this wilderness to kill this whole assembly with hunger." Then God rained "bread from heaven." This was the magical stuff called *manna*. It was delicious to eat. There was enough of it for every family in Israel, and a double amount for Shabbat.

The Arabs of Sinai give the name *manna* to a hard, honey-like juice which comes from a bush that grows in the wilderness. We cannot know for certain, but this may have been the *manna* that appeared each morning on the bushes.

A woman plays the cymbals in this ancient clay statue.

Rabbi Shmuel ben Meir used to say: God used a strong east wind to make the waters of the sea divide. In this way, the miracle was a part of nature. True miracles happen when something natural occurs at just the right time and just the right place.

All Lives are Precious

Rabban Yohanan used to say: The angels heard the Israelites singing at the Sea of Reeds, and they too wanted to sing God's praises. But God stopped them. God said, "My children, the Egyptians, are drowning in the sea. Is this a time for singing?" True, the Egyptians deserved to be destroyed, but God did not forget that their lives were precious.

God was not happy to have to destroy the Egyptians, even though they were cruel to the Israelites. God always hopes that people will stop doing evil and ask for forgiveness. God says, "I have no pleasure in the death of the wicked. Instead, the wicked should turn to good and live."
[Sources: Meg. 10b; Ezekiel 33:11; Exodus Rabbah 9:1]

12

Is this *manna?* A sweet and tasty juice is left on tamarisk bushes in the Sinai wilderness by insects.

· M · A · Z · E ·
Crossing the Sea of Reeds

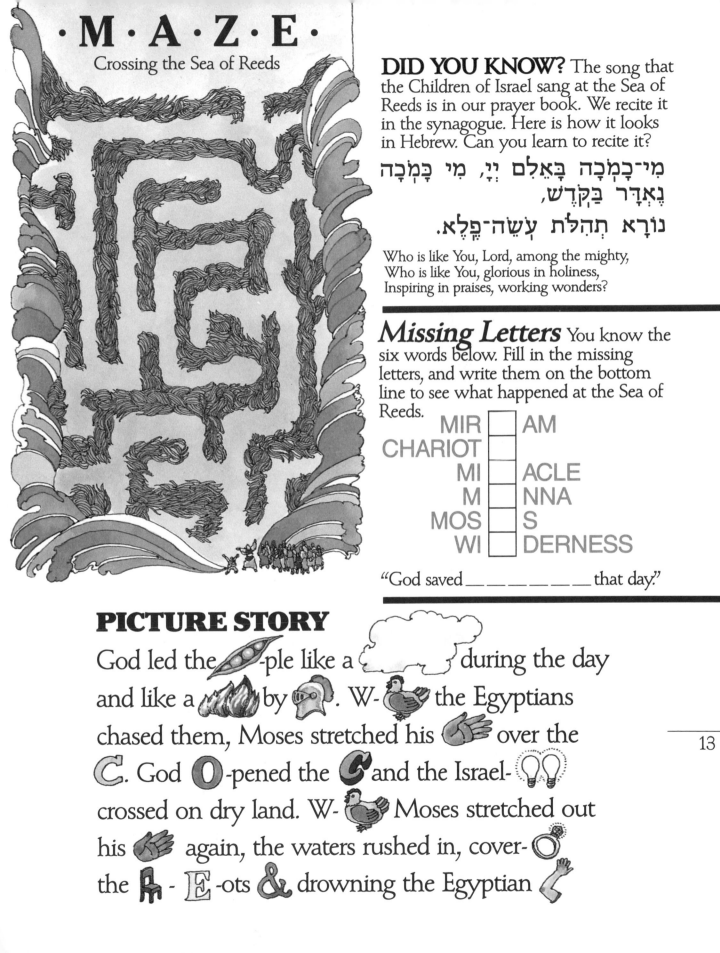

DID YOU KNOW? The song that the Children of Israel sang at the Sea of Reeds is in our prayer book. We recite it in the synagogue. Here is how it looks in Hebrew. Can you learn to recite it?

מִי־כָמֹכָה בָּאֵלִם יְיָ, מִי כָּמֹכָה
נֶאְדָּר בַּקֹּדֶשׁ,
נוֹרָא תְהִלֹּת עֹשֵׂה־פֶלֶא.

Who is like You, Lord, among the mighty,
Who is like You, glorious in holiness,
Inspiring in praises, working wonders?

Missing Letters

You know the six words below. Fill in the missing letters, and write them on the bottom line to see what happened at the Sea of Reeds.

MIR ☐ AM
CHARIOT ☐
MI ☐ ACLE
M ☐ NNA
MOS ☐ S
WI ☐ DERNESS

"God saved _ _ _ _ _ _ _ that day."

PICTURE STORY

God led the [pea]-ple like a [cloud] during the day and like a [fire] by [helmet]. W-[hen] the Egyptians chased them, Moses stretched his [hand] over the [C]. God [O]-pened the [C] and the Israel-[ites] crossed on dry land. W-[hen] Moses stretched out his [hands] again, the waters rushed in, cover-[O] the [chair]-[E]-ots & drowning the Egyptian [arm]

13

Exodus 19-34 שְׁמוֹת

Chapter 2

THE SUPREME GIFT

14

On the third new moon, the Children of Israel camped near Mount Sinai. God said to Moses, "Tell the people: I brought you here as if on the wings of eagles. If you obey My commands and keep My convenant, you will be My treasured people. The earth is Mine, but for My sake, the Children of Israel shall be a kingdom of priests, a holy nation."

On the morning of the third day, the mountain was covered in cloud. Thunder and lightning were everywhere. The people stood at the foot of the mountain and heard the powerful blast of the *shofar*. Then God came down in fire, so that all of Mount Sinai was covered in smoke like the smoke of a great furnace. The mountain shuddered as if the earth were quaking. The sound of the *shofar* grew louder and louder. And God spoke the words of the Ten Commandments.

The people were filled with terror. They said to Moses, "You speak to us and we will obey. If God speaks to us, we may die!" But Moses said, "Do not be afraid. God is testing you. You must carry the memory of God's power with you always."

God said to Moses, "Come up to Me on the mountain. I will give you the laws on tablets of stone so that you can teach them." So Moses went up on the mountain, into the cloud. For forty days and forty nights, Moses was on the mountain. Then God gave Moses the two tablets of the Covenant—tablets of stone, written by God.

Moses was gone a long time. The people gathered together against Aaron, saying, "That man Moses who brought us out of Egypt—we do not know what has happened to him. You must make us a god to lead us."

Aaron said, "Take all the golden earrings from the people and bring them to me." And Aaron melted the gold in the shape of a calf. When the people saw it, they announced, "This is your god, O Israel, that brought you out of the land of Egypt!" And the people worshipped the golden calf.

God said to Moses, "Hurry down! Your people have done evil. I will destroy Israel and make your own children into a great nation." But Moses pleaded, "Forgive the Children of Israel. Remember Abraham, Isaac, and Israel, Your servants: You promised to make their children as many as the stars of heaven. You promised them the land forever."

Now Moses went down from the mountain, and the two tablets were in his hand. As he came near, he saw the golden calf and the people dancing around it. Greatly angered, Moses heaved the tablets from his hands, breaking them at the foot of the mountain.

Moses took the calf and burned it in the fire and ground it into powder. Moses asked Aaron, "Why have you done this thing?" Aaron replied, "The people's heart was set on evil. I only tried to keep them from doing worse!"

"These people have sinned a great sin with their golden calf!" Moses said to God. "Will You forgive them?" God replied, "Whoever has sinned against Me, I will erase from My book."

And God said, "Cut two tablets of stone like the first ones. I will write on them the words that were on the first tablets which you broke." So Moses cut two tablets of stone.

Moses rose early in the morning and carried the tablets up Mount Sinai, as God commanded. Again, Moses was with God forty days and forty nights. He wrote on the tablets the words of the covenant, the Ten Commandments.

At last Moses came down from Mount Sinai, carrying the two tablets in his hand. He did not know that the skin of his face was glowing with light. Aaron and all the Children of Israel saw Moses' face and they were afraid to come near him. Yet Moses called them near and gave them all the commandments that God had spoken to him on Mount Sinai. Then Moses covered his face with a veil.

Whenever Moses went to speak with God, he took the veil from his face until after he came out to speak to the Children of Israel. And whenever the Children of Israel saw that glow in Moses' face, they knew that God had spoken to him.

And God spoke the words of the Ten Commandments.

When God made a covenant with Noah, the sign of the covenant was the rainbow. Later, in God's covenant with Abraham, the sign was circumcision. The sign of the covenant at Mount Sinai was the Ten Commandments. Here, in short, are the words which God wrote in fire on the two tablets of stone:

I am YHVH your God who brought you out of the land of Egypt, out of the House of Slavery. You shall have no other gods except Me.

You shall not make for yourself a statue or portrait of what is in the heavens above or on the earth below, or in the waters.

You shall not bow down to them or serve them.

You shall not speak God's name for a false reason.

Remember the Sabbath day, to keep it holy.

Honor your father and your mother, that your life may be long on the land that God is giving you.

A stone carving of the two tablets of the Ten Commandments.

You shall not murder.

You shall not be unfaithful to your wife or husband.

You shall not steal.

You shall not lie when you witness against your neighbor.

You shall not wish to possess a thing that belongs to your neighbor.

Three thousand carved steps lead to the top of this mountain which local people call "the Mount of Moses," thinking it may have been Mount Sinai.

17

The Golden Calf

The Ten Commandments and the golden calf teach us an important lesson about God and about ourselves. Even as God was giving Moses the tablets of the Ten Commandments on Mount Sinai, the people were making a new god. God knew this and told Moses to "Hurry down."

Some Israelites were truly evil. They turned against God entirely. Of them, God said, "Whoever has sinned against Me, I will erase from My book."

Some Israelites had not sinned. They refused to worship the golden calf. For their sake, God gave the Ten Commandments a second time.

Most of the Israelites had just slipped. They were behaving like Egyptians, making gods of gold. No human being can be perfect—not even a Moses.

God understands human beings. God knows that we are sometimes weak—that we sometimes make mistakes. Just as God gave the Ten Commandments a second time, God is willing to give us a second chance, too.

This statue reminds us of the story of the golden calf. Ancient peoples worshipped many animal gods—the snake, the jackal, the hippopotamus, and even the cow.

A LESSON ABOUT THE TORAH

The Five Books of Moses

Rabbi Joshua ben Levi used to say: After God gave the commandments to Moses at Sinai, an angel asked God, "Where are Your laws?" And God said, "I have given My laws to the Earth." So the angel went to Earth and said, "Where have you put the laws of God?" But Earth said, "I do not have them." Then the angel went to the Sea. But the Sea said, "The laws are not with me." The angel searched high and low, asking, "Where are God's laws? Who has them?" Everywhere, the answer was the same: "They are not here."

The angel said to God, "Your laws cannot be found." And God said, "Ask Moses." So the angel went to Moses and said, "Where are the laws God gave you?" But Moses answered, "I am but a small thing on the earth. Do you think that God gave the Torah to me?"

God said to Moses, "Why do you lie, saying I did not give you My Torah?"

Moses said, "O God, You placed them in my hand not for me alone, but for all people. Should I brag and say the Torah is mine?"

Then God said, "Because you do not claim this honor for yourself, I shall give you a reward. My laws shall always be called by your name." Even now, we call the Torah, "The Five Books of Moses."

[Source: Maaseh, Book 2]

No one really knows the location of Mount Sinai, but legend says it is in this mountain range in southern Sinai.

19

WORD SEARCH

Look across and down to find 14 words you know. Circle each word that you find.

```
C O M M A N D M E N T S
O L O D C A L F B S K T
V K U G O L D I C I O A
E M N E J A A R O N B B
N H T H U N D E R A E L
A O A S H O F A R I Y E
N L I G H T N I N G X T
T Y N L B A H M O S E S
```

True or False

Mark the true sentences with a "T" and put an "F" beside each one that is false.

☐ 1. God said, "The children of Israel shall be a kingdom of kings."

☐ 2. When God came down, Mount Sinai was covered in smoke.

☐ 3. The people said to Aaron, "You must make us a golden frog."

☐ 4. The people brought their gold to Aaron.

☐ 5. Moses pleaded with God, "Forgive the Children of Israel."

☐ 6. Moses broke the first two tablets, then he broke the second tablets, too.

☐ 7. When Aaron saw that glow in Moses' face, Aaron was afraid to come near Moses.

FILL IN THE BOXES Put the first letter of each word in the box below it.

Now put the letters in the correct order to finish this sentence:
"God gave Moses two ___ ___ ___ ___ ___ ___ of stone."

20

You Be The Teacher
Choose one of the Ten Commandments and use your own words to tell what it means_____

_____

_____

_____

_____

Rules to Live By

There are ten rules below. Draw a ✡ beside the two that come from the Ten Commandments.

_____1. Always make your bed when you wake in the morning.

_____2. Remember to put stamps on envelopes before mailing letters.

_____3. Don't take anything that belongs to someone else.

_____4. Do not chew gum in class.

_____5. Look both ways before crossing the street.

_____6. Remember God's promise to Noah when you see a rainbow.

_____7. Always treat teachers in a kind way.

_____8. Do not argue with your brothers, sisters, or friends.

_____9. Always try to do what your mother and father ask you to do.

_____10. Never be late for school.

OPPOSITES

Each word in the first column means the opposite of a word in the second column. Connect the opposites with lines.

LIFE	CURSE
BLESSING	TAKE
WEEP	DEATH
SHOUT	WEAK
ANGRY	WHOLE
BROKEN	WHISPER
GIVE	LAUGH
MIGHTY	PLEASED

21

Numbers 13-14; 20 בַּמִדְבָּר

Deuteronomy 30-32; 34 דְּבָרִים

Chapter 3

AN END TO WANDERING

he Lord said to Moses, "Send twelve men, one from each tribe, to spy out the land of Canaan, which I am giving to the Israelites." Moses instructed the men, "See what kind of country it is. Are the people weak or strong, few or many? Is the land good or bad? And be certain to bring back some of the fruit of the land." The men went up and spied out the land. The trees of the orchards were bursting with pomegranates and figs; and the vines bent low with the weight of their grapes. The men cut a branch with one cluster of grapes so heavy that it took two men to carry it. And they named that place The River of the Cluster.

After forty days they returned and reported to the whole community. "It is a land flowing with milk and honey, and this is its fruit. But the people there are mighty warriors and their cities are large and surrounded by heavy walls. And all the people we saw looked like the children of giants, so that we looked like grasshoppers to them!"

All that night, the people cried, "Why is God sending us to our death? Let us choose a new leader and return to Egypt!" But Joshua and Caleb, two of the spies, said, "Have no fear, the land is good and if God is good to us, God will take us into it." But the people refused to listen.

God said to Moses, "How long will it be before this people has faith in Me? Have I not done wonders for them? Say to them, 'Except for Caleb and Joshua, no one of more than twenty years shall enter this land. Your punishment shall be to wander forty years in the wilderness, one year for each day that the spies were in the land.'"

The wandering began. At Kadesh, Miriam died and was buried. The people had no water and they complained to Moses and Aaron. God said to Moses, "Take your rod and bring together the people. While they watch, you tell the rock to give water." Then Moses and Aaron gathered the congregation together before the rock. Moses said, "Can we bring water from this rock?"

The people watched him with strange looks in their eyes – terrible looks that caused Moses to worry even more. He wondered what they would do if the water did not appear, or even if there was not enough. At last, Moses struck the rock twice with his rod and water gushed out and the people and their animals drank.

Then God spoke to Moses and Aaron, "Because you did not trust Me, you shall not lead the people into the land of Canaan."

When the wandering neared its end, Moses called all Israel and said to them: "God has said, 'This command, the Torah, is not too mysterious for you, nor is it far off. It is not in heaven, nor is it beyond the sea. It is very close to you, in your mouth and in your heart, that you may do it. I command you today to love God, to walk in God's ways, and to keep God's commandments, laws, and judgments. Heaven and earth are My witnesses: I place before you life and death, the blessing and the curse; therefore choose life, that you and your children may live. Then you may dwell in the land which God swore to Abraham, Isaac, and Jacob, to give them.'"

Then Moses said to them: "I am one hundred and twenty years old today. God has told me that I shall not cross over this Jordan River. But God crosses over to lead you and Joshua crosses over to lead you. It will be as God has spoken."

God said to Moses, "Behold, the time comes when you must die." So Moses wrote the words of God's law in a book. And Moses commanded the Levites, "Take this Book of the Torah and put it beside the Ark of the Covenant."

That very same day, God spoke to Moses. "Go up Mount Nebo, across from Jericho and look out at the land of Canaan. You shall die on this mountain just as Aaron your brother died on Mount Hor."

Then Moses went up to Mount Nebo and God showed him all the land. Moses the servant of God died there and God buried him. But no one knows his grave to this day.

Moses was one hundred and twenty years old when he died. His eyes were still perfect and he still had the strength of his youth. And the Children of Israel wept for Moses thirty days. Since that time, there has never been another prophet like Moses, whom God knew face to face.

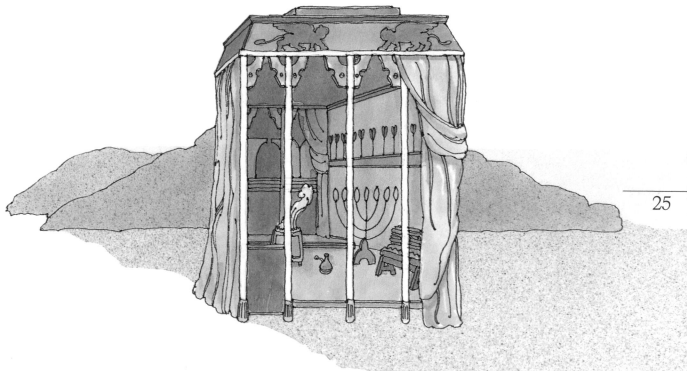

Books are precious to the Jewish people. The more we use them, the more they seem like treasured friends.

WHAT DOES IT MEAN?

"...Put it beside the Ark of the Covenant."

When Moses went up on Sinai the first time, God said, "Let the people make Me a sanctuary so that I may dwell among them." God gave instructions for making an Ark, a Tabernacle (made of tents, curtains, and altars), and a Menorah.

The Ark of the Covenant was a cabinet without legs, carried on two long poles. The Ark held the two tablets of the Ten Commandments, all the pieces of the two tablets which Moses had broken, and the Book of the Torah. Even now, at the heart of every synagogue is an Ark which holds the Torah scrolls.

Keeping the broken pieces of the first two tablets reminds us of another ancient custom which we still

observe. When prayerbooks or other holy books wear out, we do not destroy them. In older synagogues, there used to be a special room called a *genizah* where these books were kept. The word *genizah* comes from ancient Persian and means "hidden." Today, we show our love for these precious books by burying them in a cemetery.

WHAT DOES IT TEACH?

Why Moses Was Not Allowed Into the Promised Land

It seems strange that God would punish Moses by not allowing him to enter Canaan. Some say that the reason was because God told Moses to speak to the rock and ask it to give water, but Moses was angry and used his rod to strike the rock instead. Others say that the reason was that Moses lost his faith in God for a moment, asking, "Can we bring water from this rock?" But both of these seem like small matters.

This oasis may be the biblical Rephidim where Moses struck the rock instead of speaking to it as God commanded.

When a person becomes great, and many people depend on him or her, that person must not fail even in little ways. All the people looked to Moses to tell them exactly what God wanted. Even his smallest mistake could hurt the people. So Moses was punished for not doing exactly as God commanded.

A LESSON FROM THE PROPHETS
The Book of Joshua

When Moses died, he left behind a strong leader, Joshua bin Nun. His story is told in the Book of Joshua, the first book in the section of the Bible called The Prophets.

Joshua led the people into many battles. The most famous took place at Jericho, the city which Moses saw from Mount Nebo. Jericho is famous for being the oldest city in the world. It was built like a fort, enclosed in heavy walls. It seemed that it would take a miracle to conquer it. Here is the story:

> The gates of Jericho were sealed. None went out, and none came in. And God said to Joshua, "See! I give Jericho into your hand. Send all your men of war to march around the city for six days. Let seven priests carry *shofars* before the Ark. On the seventh day, march around the city seven times with the priests blowing the *shofars.* And when they sound a long blast, let all the people shout. Then the wall of the city will fall down flat."

Now Joshua told the people, "Do not shout or make any noise with your voice, until the day I say to you, 'Shout!' Then you shall shout." So they did, for six days.

But on the seventh day they marched around the city seven times. And the seventh time, when the priests blew the shofars, Joshua cried out, "Shout! God has given you the city!"

So the people shouted and the wall fell down flat. Then the people took the city. God was with Joshua, and his fame spread throughout all the country.

[Source: Joshua, 6]

Today, as in the days of the spies, grapes grow throughout the Land of Israel.

Buried deep beneath the earth, archaeologists found this stone tower. Once it was part of the town wall of Jericho, the world's first city.

27

MYSTERY NAME

Cross out any letter that appears two times. Copy the remaining letters in the line below to find the mystery name.

J K I B O D L E C S
Y L W P M W T P I Y
H T B E C U K M D A

WAS A STRONG LEADER WHO LED THE PEOPLE INTO MANY BATTLES.

Fill in the Blanks

Moses called the people together to tell them what God had said. Use the words below to complete the story.

COMMAND   PLACE   WALK   KEEP   LOVE
LAWS   BLESSING   LIFE   CHOOSE   CHILDREN

God has said, "I _____ you today to _____ God, to _____ in God's ways, and to _____ God's commandments, _____ and judgements. I _____ before you _____ and death, the _____ and the curse; therefore _____ life, that you and your _____ may live."

NAME THAT PLACE

1. The people wanted to return to _____.
2. Miriam was buried at _____.
3. Aaron died on _____.
4. Moses was buried on _____.
5. Joshua marched around the wall of the city of _____.

28

LOOKING FOR UNDERSTANDING

Circle the best answer.

1. Moses sent twelve men, one from each tribe, to
   - buy fruit.
   - spy out the land of Canaan.
   - find water.

2. The Ark of the Covenant was
   - left in the wilderness.
   - carried on two long poles.
   - given to the spies.

3. The cluster of grapes was so heavy that
   - the spies could not carry it.
   - it took two spies to carry it.
   - the spies left it on the vine.

4. Moses worried that the rock
   - would crumble when he hit it.
   - would hit him back if he hit it.
   - would not give water for the people.

5. The people of the land looked like giants and the spies
   - looked like ants to them.
   - looked like they were lost.
   - looked like grasshoppers.

6. The Ark of the Covenant was filled with
   - the Torah and the tablets.
   - memories of the land of Egypt.
   - bread and manna.

7. Moses was not allowed to
   - tell stories to the people.
   - teach Torah to the people.
   - enter the Promised Land.

8. To this day, no one knows
   - why the people made a Golden Calf.
   - where Moses was buried.
   - how the land came to be called Israel.

9. God told the people
   - to choose sides.
   - to choose life.
   - to choose nice homes.

Numbers

Can you complete each sentence with the correct number?

1. God gave _____ Commandments.

2. God said that no one older than _____ years old shall enter the land.

3. God said that the punishment would be to wander in the wilderness for _____ years.

4. Moses struck the rock with his rod _____ times.

5. Moses lived for _____ years.

6. Joshua and the people marched around Jericho _____ times.

Joshua 23-24 יְהוֹשֻעַ

Judges 2-5 שׁוֹפְטִים

Chapter 4

DEBORAH JUDGES ISRAEL

Many years passed. The people settled in the Land of Israel and for a while, all was peaceful. Then Joshua called the Israelites together at Shechem. Joshua said, "I have grown old. Soon I must die. You have seen what God has done for you. Because God fights for you, each of you is like a thousand warriors." Then Joshua repeated their history. He told them about Abraham, Jacob and Joseph, and about the years of wandering. Joshua asked, "Do you promise to serve God always?" And the people said, "We will serve only God. We will obey only God."

30

On that day, Joshua made a covenant with the people. He wrote all this in a book of God's teachings. He set up a great stone at Shechem to be the sign of the covenant between God and Israel.

Then Joshua, the servant of God, died at the age of one hundred and ten years. And the people of Israel buried him on his own farm in the Land of Israel. The people served God as they had promised, for they had seen the mighty deeds which God had done for them. But their children had not seen these marvels, and soon they began to worship foreign gods. So the enemies of Israel grew stronger.

Then God gave Israel Judges to lead them against their enemies. And God was with the Judges while they lived. Yet, when the Judges died, the people would grow weak and forget God again, bowing down to idols. So it was, for many years, as God tested the Israelites.

In time, the prophetess Deborah was made Judge over Israel. She sat beneath the palm tree of Deborah between Ramah and Beth-El in the mountains of Ephraim. And whenever the Children of Israel had an argument, they came to her to be judged.

Once she sent for the famous soldier, Barak, and said to him, "God has commanded you to go to Mount Tabor. There you will battle against Sisera, who commands the great army of Jabin, with all its chariots. Fear not, for God will defeat them." Barak said, "If you will go with me, then I will go. But if you will not go with me, I will not go."

"I will surely go with you," Deborah answered. "But know this: God will not let you kill Sisera. Sisera will fall at the hand of a woman."

Now Sisera had nine hundred chariots of iron, and all his army. Barak's army was all on foot, and their weapons were few. So it was God who defeated Sisera and all his chariots and all his army. And of all his mighty army, only Sisera escaped.

Sisera ran to the tent of Yael, the wife of Heber, a friend of King Jabin. And Yael said, "You can rest here with me." She brought him into the tent and covered him with a blanket. He said, "Stand at the door of the tent. If anyone asks, 'Is there a man here?' you shall say, 'No.'"

But when Sisera was asleep, Yael took a tent peg and a hammer and went softly to his bed. Then she drove the peg into the side of his head. So Sisera died.

Yael came out of the tent and saw Barak. She knew that he was looking for Sisera. "Come," she said, "I will show you the man you seek." And when he went into her tent, there he saw the dead Sisera. That is how God destroyed the army of Jabin, king of Canaan.

Then Deborah and Barak sang on that day:

Hear, O kings!
    Give ear, O princes!
I, even I, will sing to God.
    I will sing praise to the God of Israel.

And the land was peaceful again for forty years.

Here at Mount Tabor, Deborah and Barak defeated the army of Sisera.

WHAT DOES IT MEAN?

God gave Israel judges...

Jethro – the priest of Midian and the father-in-law of Moses – joined Moses in the wilderness. He saw Moses judging the Israelites from morning to night.

Jethro said, "Moses, this is not right. You must find judges among the people to share the work of judging." Moses liked Jethro's idea, and he set many judges over Israel. Then Jethro said, "Now I will leave you."

Moses was sad, "Stay with me, please," he said. "I need you and I need your wonderful ideas."

"I am only a lamp," Jethro answered, "but you are the sun and Aaron is the moon. Where the sun and moon give light, no lamp is needed. I must return to my people and teach them God's ways. The lamp is best in a place of darkness."

WHAT DOES IT TEACH?

Deborah
The Prophetess

The Bible calls three women by the title prophetess: Miriam, Deborah, and Huldah. Miriam was the sister of Moses. She looked after the baby Moses and later helped her brother lead the Israelites. At the Sea of Reeds, Miriam led Israel in singing and dancing when the Egyptians were drowned.

Deborah lived one hundred and fifty years after Joshua. She judged Israel for many years, and all the people loved her. Barak knew that the people would follow Deborah into battle. For that reason, Barak asked Deborah to join him in leading the army.

Huldah was a prophetess in Jerusalem long after Deborah's time. When King Josiah found the Book of the Torah after it had been lost for many years, Huldah spoke God's words to the king.

The rabbis taught: It makes no difference if a person is a man or a woman – God's spirit enters the person who follows God's ways.

The palm tree on this ancient Jewish coin was used as a symbol of the Land of Israel.

33

A LESSON FROM THE PROPHETS

The Book of Judges

Local legend says that Joshua was buried here, near the city of Shechem.

Joshua brought the Ark of the Covenant and the Tabernacle to Shiloh. The Children of Israel divided the land, giving each tribe a portion. But the tribes seldom went to Shiloh. They worshipped near home. In the north, they worshipped at Dan. In the center of the country, they worshipped at Shechem, Shiloh, or Gilgal. And in the south, they worshipped at Hebron or Beersheba. In each place, they worshipped "the God of Israel," but they did not think of themselves as one people.

"Then God gave Israel judges…" When a tribe was attacked by an enemy, other tribes came to help in the battle. (When Deborah called, Barak's army came from the tribes of Naftali and Zebulun.) The leaders who brought the tribes together were called "judges." Some, like Deborah beneath her palm tree, also settled arguments. Perhaps that is why they were called judges.

The Book of Judges tells the story of twelve leaders. Deborah was the only woman, but she was one of the three most important judges. The other two were Gideon and Samson. From first to last, the judges were favorites of the people, ruling because the people wanted them to rule.

[Sources: Joshua, 13ff.; Judges]

These three sealed-up gates in the walls of Jerusalem are called the Huldah Gates. It is said that Huldah trained prophets nearby.

34

NAME SCRAMBLE

Unscramble the letters to see the names of people you have read about.

O S J H A U _____

O S M S E _____

B H A R A M A _____

C A J B O _____

S E J O P H _____

E T H J O R _____

B E R H A D O _____

K A B A R _____

E S I S A R _____

A B J N I _____

A Y L E _____

THE CORRECT ORDER

All these things happened in the story, but they are not in the right order.
Number the sentences in the order that they happened.

_____ When the Children of Israel had an argument, they came to Deborah to be judged.

_____ Joshua called the Israelites together at Shechem.

_____ Barak defeated the great army of Jabin.

_____ Joshua set up a stone to be the sign of the covenant between God and Israel.

_____ God gave Israel judges to lead them against their enemies.

_____ Yael killed Sisera while he lay sleeping.

35

What happened when Joshua called the Israelites together at Shechem?

_____

What happened when the Children of Israel had an argument?

_____

What happened when the Judges died?

_____

What happened when the people began to worship foreign gods?

_____

What happened when Deborah sent for Barak?

_____

What happened when Sisera escaped?

_____

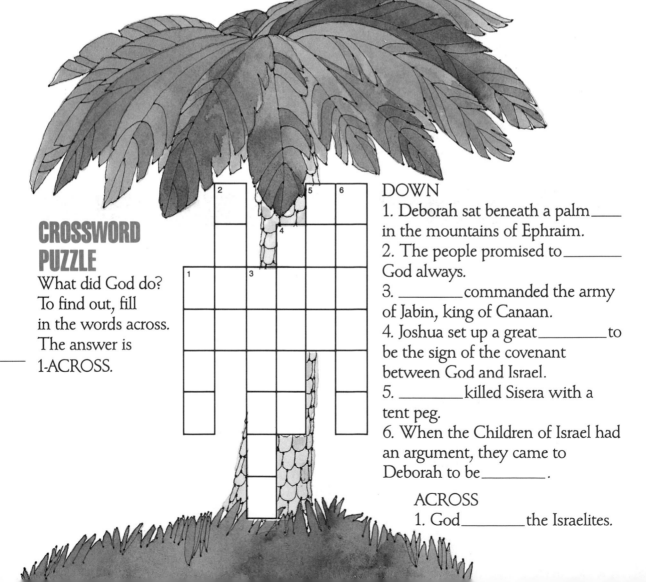

CROSSWORD PUZZLE

What did God do?
To find out, fill
in the words across.
The answer is
1-ACROSS.

DOWN
1. Deborah sat beneath a palm_____ in the mountains of Ephraim.
2. The people promised to_____ God always.
3. _____commanded the army of Jabin, king of Canaan.
4. Joshua set up a great_____to be the sign of the covenant between God and Israel.
5. _____killed Sisera with a tent peg.
6. When the Children of Israel had an argument, they came to Deborah to be_____.

ACROSS
1. God_____the Israelites.

WHAT IS TRUE?

Put a T in each box next to a true statement. Put an F in each box next to a statement which is false.

- [ ] Joshua died at the age of ninety-eight.
- [ ] Joshua made a covenant with the people.
- [ ] Jethro told Moses to hire many leaders for the people.
- [ ] Deborah sat beneath a palm tree in the mountains.
- [ ] Barak killed Sisera with a tent peg.
- [ ] Jabin's army had no chariots.
- [ ] Deborah went with Barak to lead the people in battle.
- [ ] Sisera asked Yael to kill Barak and Deborah.
- [ ] Yael sang a song to God.
- [ ] After Deborah, the land was peaceful for forty years.

Judges 6-8 שׁוֹפְטִים

Chapter 5

GIDEON AND THE TRICK

Whenever the farmers of Israel harvested their grain, raiders called the Midianites attacked. The Midianites came down on them like locusts—they and their camels without number—and they stole the Israelites' grain. In their hunger, the Children of Israel cried out to God.

To hide his grain from the Midianites, Gideon did his threshing in the winepress instead of on top of a hill. Once, while he was threshing wheat, an angel of God appeared. The angel said to Gideon, "God is with you, you mighty man of valor!"

Gideon said, "O my lord, if God is with us, where are God's miracles now? Truly, God has forgotten us and given us to the Midianites."

Then God turned to Gideon and said, "You are mighty and I will be with you. Even by yourself, you can defeat the Midianites!"

Just then, the Midianites and other raiders called the Amalekites gathered together and camped in the Valley of Jezreel. But Gideon felt the Spirit of God within him. He blew the *shofar,* and the men of the city of Abiezer joined him. He sent messengers to the tribes of Manasseh, Asher, Zebulun, and Naphtali. And they all came to join him.

Then Gideon and all his followers camped beside Ein Harod, near the camp of the Midianites. And God said to Gideon, "You have too many people with you. If I let them defeat the Midianites now, the Israelites will say they won by their own strength. Go and tell the people, 'Whoever is fearful and afraid, let him leave at once.'" And twenty-two thousand men left, and ten thousand remained.

39

And God said to Gideon, "There are still too many. Bring them down to the water, and I will test them for you." So Gideon brought the people down to the water. And God said to Gideon, "Divide the people who drink like dogs—lapping water with their tongues—from those who get down on their knees to drink." And three hundred men lapped the water as they drank, while the rest got down on their knees to drink water.

God said to Gideon, "The three hundred men who lapped are enough." And Gideon sent away all but the three hundred men. That very night, God said to Gideon, "Rise up, go down against the camp of Midian, for I am defeating them for you."

Then Gideon divided the men into three groups. He put a *shofar* in each man's hand, and gave each man a pitcher with a torch. He said to them, "Do as I do. When I blow the *shofar*, you also blow the *shofar*, and shout out, 'The sword of God and of Gideon!'"

So Gideon and his group came to the Midianite camp in the middle of the night. And they blew the *shofar*s and broke the pitchers that were in their hands. And on three sides, the groups blew the *shofar*s and smashed the pitchers. Then they held the torches in their left hands and the *shofar*s in their right hands for blowing. And they cried, "The sword of God and of Gideon!"

The Israelites stood still all around the camp. And God confused the Midianites so that everywhere in the camp, men drew their swords, killing one another. Then the Midianite army cried out and fled.

Gideon sent messengers in every direction, saying, "Go out to battle against the Midianites and drive them out of the land." And Gideon led his three hundred men across the Jordan. There he found fifteen thousand Midianites, all who were left, for one hundred and twenty thousand had been slain. And Gideon attacked the army as it rested. So Gideon defeated the Midianites.

Then the people of Israel said to Gideon, "Rule over us, both you and your son, and your grandson also. For you have saved us from the Midianites." But Gideon said, "I will not rule over you, nor shall my son rule over you. God shall rule over you."

So the country was at peace for forty years in the days of Gideon.

An ancient stone carving shows a man blowing a horn trumpet. Gideon's men blew *shofar*s to startle and confuse the sleeping Midianites.

called "angels" since they were the messengers of God.

The angel calls Gideon a "mighty man of valor." This helps Gideon get ready to hear God's voice asking him to go to war. In the same way, Moses first saw the burning bush, then heard God's voice telling him to go to Egypt.

Gideon led his soldiers across the Jordan River to destroy the Midianite army.

WHAT DOES IT MEAN?

...An angel of God appeared.

First an angel spoke with Gideon and then, a moment later, God spoke to Gideon directly. The mystery is, why did God send the angel first? The answer may be found in the Hebrew word for angel, *mal'ach*.

The word *mal'ach* means both "angel" and "messenger." At times the Bible uses the word to mean a human messenger. So the Torah says, "God... sent an angel and brought us out of Egypt." This "angel" was Moses. And the prophets of Israel were also

Our sages say: God has placed each of us in this world for a special purpose. But how will you know what God wants you to do? One day—any day—you may hear a messenger. It could be a parent or a teacher or a friend. Whoever it is, he or she will help you know what you can do. Afterward, when you help others, you must act as if your decision truly came from heaven. You must feel commanded.

41

Judah, the leader of the Maccabees. A Jewish artist, living some 1600 years after the Maccabees, drew this picture by imagining how Judah might have looked.

WHAT DOES IT TEACH?

Gideon Would Not Be King

When Gideon defeated the Midianites, the Israelites asked him to be their king. Gideon must have thought long and hard about this. It is a great honor to be asked to be a king. Almost anyone would want that kind of honor. But, in the end, Gideon chose peace for himself and peace for all Israel. He said, "God shall rule over you."

Once, Alexander the Great, one of the most famous of all kings, was proudly returning from a great victory. As he rode his white horse, a townsman stopped him. The man said, "O mighty king, it is good that you won the little war!"

"What war is greater than the one I won?" Alexander asked.

The townsman explained, "The great war is the war against the evil inside you. Peace for the world begins with peace inside yourself."

Clay pot from a Midianite temple at Timna. At one time, the Midianites were fine potters.

A LESSON FROM THE PROPHETS

Not by Might, Not by Power

Gideon's defeat of the huge army of Midian with just three hundred men reminds us of the story of Hanukkah. With a small army of farmers, the Maccabees defeated the mighty armies of the Syrian Greeks. They took Jerusalem and cleaned the Temple, smashing the Greek idols. Like Gideon, the Maccabees trusted in God. The name Maccabee may come from the initials of four words in the song Miriam sang at the Sea of Reeds, *Mi chamocha ba-elim YHVH?*, "Who is like You, O God, among the gods?"

Every week we read a section from the Books of the Prophets in the synagogue. This section is called the *haftarah*. The *haftarah* for the Sabbath of Hanukkah comes from the Book of Zechariah. It tells how the rabbis felt about the celebration of Hanukkah: "Not by might, not by power, but by [God's] Spirit [shall you win over your enemies]." This is the same message that we find in the story of Gideon.

[Sources: Judges 5:1-31; Zechariah 4:6]

Choose the Best

Circle the words that best complete the sentence.

1

Whenever the people of Israel harvested grain,
the grasshoppers ate it.
they blew the *shofar.*
the Midianites attacked.

2

When Gideon sent messengers to other tribes to come and fight,
they were all thirsty.
a king was chosen.
they all came to join him.

3

When God confused the Midianites,
they forgot their names.
the soldiers killed one another.
they counted their camels.

4

After the battle, the Israelites said to Gideon,
"That was great, let's fight some more!"
"We want you to rule over us."
"We want God to rule over us."

5

Gideon gave each soldier
a post card from home.
a bell, a candle, and a book.
a pitcher, a *shofar,* and a torch.

6

God told Gideon to divide the people who lapped water like dogs
from those who got down on their knees to drink.
from those who took their water from a pitcher.
from those who watered their lawns.

DO YOU KNOW WHY?

1. God said that Gideon had too many people with him because

2. The Midianites killed one another because

3. Gideon said, "God has given us to the Midianites" because

4. Gideon sent messengers in every direction because

5. The people asked Gideon to be their king because

Help Gideon find the Midianites who hid across the Jordan River.

HIDDEN PICTURES

DECODE THE MESSAGE

The secret message below is written in code. Circle every third letter to read what the angel said to Gideon.

A C G J M O T K D L N I H
P S R E W U Z I X F T G V
H B W Y S T O D Q U K L Y
A J O I X U N W M H P I L
C G U K H R W T S X Y O B
M P G A C D N I V O E Q F
N Z V N Y A T E L B G O A
H R

The angel said, "__ __ __   __ __   __ __ __ __ __

__ __ __,   __ __ __   __ __ __ __ __ __   __ __ __

__ __   __ __ __ __ __ __!"

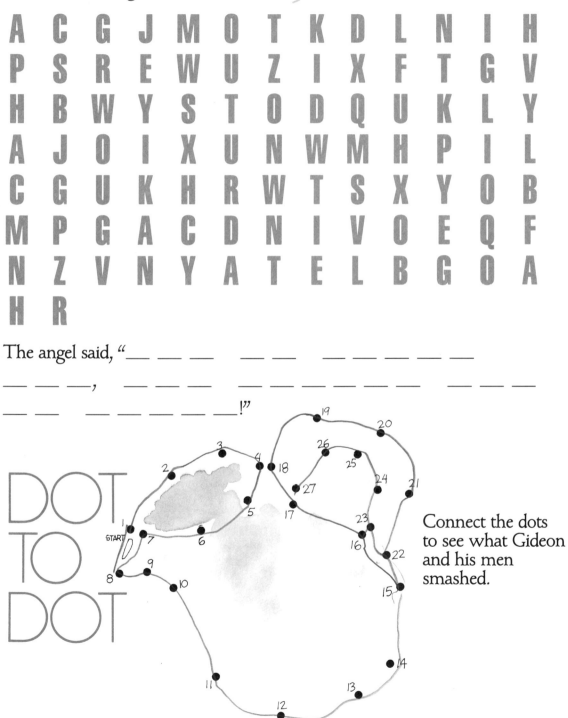

DOT
TO
DOT

Connect the dots to see what Gideon and his men smashed.

45

Judges 13-16 שׁוֹפְטִים

Chapter 6

SAMSON

gain the Children of Israel worshipped idols. And the Philistines troubled them for forty years. Manoah and his wife lived in those days, and they had no children. An angel of God came and said to the woman, "You shall soon have a son. Do not cut his hair, for he shall be a Nazirite, a man dedicated to serving God. He will begin to save Israel from the Philistines." And the woman had a son and called him Samson. Samson grew to be a man, and God's Spirit moved him.

Samson loved a Philistine woman and wanted to marry her. His parents were unhappy, but Samson married her anyway.

It was not long before Samson and his new wife quarrelled. Samson was angry. He left his wife and her father. But when Samson returned to bring his wife a present, her father said, "I thought you hated her, so I gave her to another man."

"Now," thought Samson, "I have reason to take revenge on the Philistines!" Samson captured three hundred foxes. Putting them in pairs — tail to tail — he tied a torch to each pair. When the torches were blaz-

ing, he sent the foxes running in the fields. The grain of the Philistines was burned, and so were their vineyards and olive trees.

The Philistines said, "Samson did this because his wife was given to another man." So they burned Samson's wife and her father. And Samson cried, "You have done evil and I will make you pay." He ran among the Philistines, raging like the foxes, killing many. Then he fled and hid.

The Philistines told the men of Judah, "Give us Samson, so that we may take revenge on him." And three thousand men of Judah came to Samson. "What have you done to us? Now we must give you to the Philistines." And they tied him with two new ropes.

When the Philistines saw Samson, they came shouting against him. Then the Spirit of God became Samson's strength. The ropes on his arms were like burned strips of cloth falling apart. On the ground, Samson found the jawbone of a dead donkey. He took it in his hand and swung it until a thousand Philistines lay dead. And Samson said: "With a donkey's jawbone, I have slain a thousand men!"

And Samson judged Israel for twenty years.

Afterward, Samson loved a woman named Delilah. The Philistines said to her, "Find out why Samson is so strong. Tell us how to defeat him, and we will each give you eleven hundred pieces of silver."

Delilah said to Samson, "I beg you, tell me the secret of your great strength." She pestered him daily until Samson grew tired of her begging. Then he opened his heart, and told her, "My hair has never been cut. My strength comes from my hair which I have dedicated to God. Without it, I would be like any other man."

Now Delilah sent for the Philistines and they had the money in their hands. She lulled Samson to sleep on her knees and called a man to come and cut off his hair. Then she shouted, "The Philistines are here, Samson!" He awoke to fight the Philistines, but it was too late. God's strength was gone.

The Philistines put out Samson's eyes, and took him to Gaza. In prison, they forced him to turn the stone grinding wheel, as if he were a donkey.

Yet, day by day, Samson's hair grew longer.

The Philistines made a great feast and worshipped Dagon, their god. They said: "Dagon has given us Samson, our enemy!" They brought Samson from the prison to laugh at him. Their temple was full of men, and women and three thousand more watched from the temple's roof. All the leaders of the Philistines were there. And they tied Samson between the pillars of the temple.

Then Samson said to the lad who held his hand, "Put my hands on the pillars of the temple, so that I can lean on them." And Samson spoke to God. "O God, give me strength, I pray, just this once. Let me take one revenge on the Philistines for my two eyes!"

Samson put his hands on the two pillars, shouting, "Let me die with the Philistines!" He pushed with all his might. The stone columns moved slowly outward. There was a groaning noise as they broke loose, then a shrieking cry from the people as the walls crumbled. And the temple fell upon the Philistines. By his death, Samson killed more Philistines than he had killed in his life.

And Samson judged Israel for twenty years.

What does your name mean? Our names are the first gifts that our parents give us. We can turn them into badges of honor by doing good things.

WHAT DOES IT MEAN?

An angel of God came...

The sages say that when Samson's father Manoah met the angel of God, he asked the angel's name. The angel said, "My name has no meaning for you." Human beings need names, but angels do not. Angels are God's messengers. They can appear as wind or fire, or any living thing. When the message they bear is delivered, they disappear, simply vanishing. The angel that met Manoah rose up to heaven in a flame.

We use names to help us understand people and things, to help us tell them apart from one another. So, in the story of the Garden of Eden, God brought all the animals before Adam, and Adam named each one. But God does not need names. God knows all things—living or not—from the inside out.

In the same way, God's true name has no meaning for us. God knows us through and through, but we can never know all there is to know about God.

Above: Samson was born in this gently-rolling hill-country. *Left:* Face mask of a Philistine. Clay masks were often placed on the lids of coffins.

50

Twenty Years?
Or Forty Years?

When the Bible repeats a thing twice, it must be important. But why repeat, "And Samson judged Israel for twenty years?"

Our sages taught that Samson judged twenty years when he was alive. Then, they said, Samson was still remembered and loved for a full twenty years after he died. That is why the statement is made twice.

We Jews believe that the good deeds we do live on even after we die. The world is changed because we lived in it. Our good deeds add to the good that is already in the world. The good things we say are repeated by others. They stay in the hearts and minds of the people who love us. This idea is old, very old, going all the way back to the days of the Bible.

Samson's Hair

Samson was a Nazirite. The Nazirites were a group of Jews who pledged to spend their lives adding to the holiness of the world. They wanted to be God's special servants. They set themselves apart by not drinking wine or eating meat, and by not cutting their hair. These were the signs of their covenant with God.

Samson's strength was not really in his hair. It was in the reason that he did not cut his hair. His hair was just a sign. Unfortunately, even Samson forgot this. When he gave Delilah the secret, he was really saying that his secret was his dedication to God.

Without his eyes, Samson saw more clearly. He remembered where his strength really came from. So he prayed to God to give him his strength one last time. And, with God's help, he tore down the temple of the Philistines.

Every covenant has a sign as a reminder. But we must not confuse the sign with the covenant itself. The two stone tablets remind us of the Ten Commandments, but it is up to us to remember what the commandments are.

[Source: Judges 13:4;15:7;17:28]

The desert fox of Israel. Can you remember how Samson used foxes to destroy the fields of the Philistines?

51

BIBLE DICTIONARY

Do you know what these words mean? Write a short definition under each word.

COVENANT

IDOL

MANNA

SIN

ARK OF THE COVENANT

SHOFAR

BLESSING

RIDDLES

On the way to his wedding, Samson saw the dead body of a lion. Some bees had built a hive in the lion's bones, and were making honey. Later, Samson entertained the wedding guests by telling them this riddle:

> Out of the eater came something to eat. And out of the strong came something sweet. What are they?

Of course, the answer was the lion and the honey. See if you can match the riddles with their answers below. Put the number of the answer in the box. Have fun!

RIDDLE

How many Jewish men were born during the forty years of wandering in the wilderness?

Pharaoh's daughter found Moses in a basket floating in the Nile River. What was the longest river in Egypt before the Nile was discovered.

God sent the Israelites manna to eat. If there had been no manna, what would they have eaten in the desert?

Where did the Midianites keep their armies?

The army of Jabin had many horse-drawn chariots. How do you get down from a horse?

Samson sent the foxes with the torches tied to their tails running in the Philistine fields. How do you make a slow fox fast?

ANSWER
1. Stop feeding him.
2. None. Only babies were born there.
3. You can't get down from a horse. You get down from a duck!
4. The Nile, of course!
5. In their sleevies.
6. The sand which is there.

Connections

These words will remind you of people in the Bible.
Connect the words to the correct people.

GRAPES

PALM TREE

HAND DRUM

TABLETS OF LAW

TENT PEG

CHARIOT

JERICHO

JAWBONE OF DONKEY

BROKEN PITCHER

PEOPLE
- MIRIAM
- PHARAOH
- JOSHUA
- 12 SPIES
- DEBORAH
- MOSES
- SAMSON
- YAEL
- GIDEON

Review Quiz

Put a T in the box before a true statement. Put an F in the box before a false statement.

- T   1. God gave Israel judges to lead them against their enemies.
- T   2. No one knows the place where Moses was buried.
- T   3. Gideon did not want to become a king.
- F   4. Miriam sang and danced at the Sea of Reeds.
- F   5. The Egyptians crossed the Sea of Reeds on dry ground.
- F   6. Samson's strength came from the ropes on his arms.
- T   7. God made a covenant with the people at Mount Sinai.
- F   8. Gideon told Delilah that his strength was in his hair.
- F   9. Moses was punished because he spoke to the rock instead of hitting it.
- T   10. Together, Deborah and Barak led the people into battle.
- T   11. Aaron helped the people make a Golden Calf to worship.
- F   12. Samson tied pitchers to the tails of foxes and set them loose.

53

Chapter 7

THE SCROLL OF RUTH

In the days of the judges, a man named Elimelech took his wife Naomi and their two sons to the land of Moab. Elimelech died there. His sons grew up and married two women of Moab – Orpah and Ruth. Ten years passed. Then both sons died, too. Naomi was left alone with her two daughters-in-law.

Naomi decided to return to Israel. She and her daughters-in-law started out together. Then Naomi said, "Turn back and go to your homes." She kissed them, and all three women began to weep.

Ruth and Orpah said, "Let us go with you, to your people." But Naomi repeated, "Turn back." Orpah kissed Naomi and returned to her home.

But Ruth refused to turn back. She said to Naomi, "Do not ask me to leave you. Wherever you go, I will go. Wherever you make your home, I will make my home. Your people shall be my people. And your God shall be my God. Where you die, I will die, and there I will be buried."

It was the season of the harvest when Naomi and Ruth arrived in Bethlehem. Naomi had a relative there, a man of great wealth. His name was Boaz. But Ruth and Naomi were poor and they had no food.

Ruth said, "The Torah says that the poor may glean in the fields, collecting grain that the workers leave behind. I will go out and glean so that we may have food to eat."

55

Now the first day that she went out to glean, Boaz came to his field and saw Ruth. Boaz asked his chief servant, "Who is this young woman?" And the chief servant replied, "She is the one who returned with Naomi from the land of Moab."

Then Boaz went to Ruth and said, "Stay here in my field. Do not glean in any other. I have heard how you left your parents and your land to come here. Now God will reward you."

When it was time to eat, Boaz invited Ruth to share his food. And Ruth ate, but she saved some of the food for her mother-in-law, Naomi.

Boaz instructed his workers, "Be sure to let grain slip from your hands so that she may find plenty to collect." Ruth gleaned until evening, and brought the grain and the food she had saved to Naomi.

When Naomi saw all the grain, she asked, "Where did you work?" and Ruth answered, "In the field of Boaz." Naomi thanked God and explained to Ruth that Boaz was her relative.

Every day, until the harvest was over, Ruth went to the field of Boaz. And every night she returned to Naomi.

Then Naomi said to Ruth, "My daughter, you need a home. Do as I say: Put on your best clothing and your perfumed oil. Find Boaz and wait until he lies down. Then go to him. He will tell you what you should do." And Ruth said, "I will do all you say."

After Boaz ate, his heart was cheerful, and he went to lie down. Ruth came softly, and lay down. But at midnight Boaz awoke and turned and saw her lying at his feet. "Who are you?" he asked. Ruth answered, "I am your relative, Ruth. I need your help."

Boaz said, "Do not fear. I will help you." In the morning, he gave her six measures of barley, saying, "Do not return empty-handed to your mother-in-law."

Boaz went to the city gate to find Naomi's closest relative. He said to the man, "Sit here with me." He also asked ten leaders of the city to sit with them. Boaz said to the man, "Naomi needs to sell the land of our cousin, Elimelech. Only you or I can buy it. If you do not buy it, I will." And the man said, "I will buy it."

Boaz said, "Then you must follow the law. On the day you buy the land, you must also marry Ruth of Moab. You must give her children so that her family's name will be remembered in Israel."

Then the man said, "In that case, I cannot buy it. You may take my place." As a sign of passing the land to Boaz, the man took off his sandal and gave it to Boaz.

Boaz said to the leaders, "You are my witnesses. I have bought the land. I will marry Ruth the Moabitess and give her children, to carry on her family name.

And all the people at the gate said, "May God make your wife like Rachel and Leah, who built the house of Israel."

So Boaz married Ruth. And God blessed their marriage by giving them a child.

The women said to Naomi, "Praise God! May your grandchild bring you the pleasure you lost when your sons died." Naomi loved her grandchild as if he were her own. And the neighbor women named the child Obed.

Now Obed was the father of Jesse. And Jesse was the father of David, who rose to be King of Israel.

An important archaeological find, this ancient tablet is a farmer's calendar, telling the best months for planting and reaping.

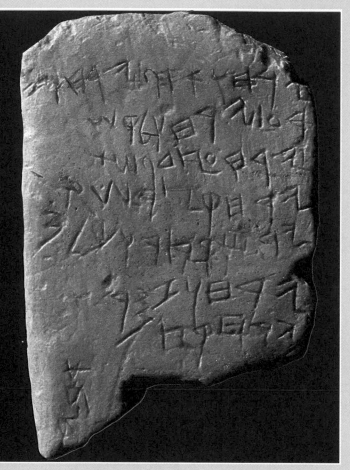

The Scroll of Ruth shows us *tzedakah* in action. Boaz was rich. Ruth and Naomi were poor. But the laws of the Torah made things more equal.

Since most Israelites were farmers, the Torah used the harvest as a way that the rich could help the poor. The corners of a field were left for the poor to harvest. And the poor could also follow the workers and collect any grain that fell from their hands. This is called "gleaning."

Today, most of us are not farmers. So we set aside a part of our money or our possessions, and give them to the poor. Our community helps to feed the hungry and take care of those who are in need. These things are also *tzedakah* in action.

The poor still glean in the fields around Bethlehem, just as they did in the days of Ruth and Naomi.

WHAT DOES IT MEAN?

"I will glean in the fields..."

58

The story of Ruth paints a picture of life at the time of the Judges. It is sometimes said that Ruth and Boaz lived while Gideon was judging Israel. In this one story, we learn about Jews and non-Jews, laws and customs, rich and poor.

View of the city of Bethlehem. The mountains of Moab—Ruth's family home—rise up in the background.

WHAT DOES IT TEACH?
Do Not Ask Me to Leave You

Naomi told Ruth and Orpah to return to their parents, their lands, and their gods. But Ruth refused to leave. Ruth loved Naomi, of course. But there was another reason: Ruth wanted to be a Jew.

Naomi said, "As a Jew, you cannot go to the great feasts at the temples of the idols." Ruth answered, "Wherever you go, I will go." Naomi said, "As a Jew, you cannot live in a house that has no *mezuzah.*" Ruth said, "Wherever you make your home, I will make my home." Naomi said, "As a Jew, you must obey the laws and keep the covenant made at Sinai." Ruth said, "Your people shall be my people, and your God shall be my God." Then Naomi taught Ruth the Torah and Ruth became a Jew.

A LESSON FROM THE PROPHETS
The Family of David

The Scroll of Ruth is one of five books in the Bible which are called "scrolls." It ends by telling us that Ruth and Boaz were the great-grandparents of King David. This is no accident. It is a great teaching. Our teachers say that Ruth lived long enough to see both David and his son Solomon become kings.

Naomi's closest relative refused to marry Ruth. He said, "I do not want my children to be the children of a convert." A convert is a person like Ruth who is born a non-Jew, but chooses to become a Jew. Our teachers say that the name of Naomi's closest relative was not even mentioned in the Bible because he did not understand the laws of the Torah.

Boaz, on the other hand, was rich in money and learning. He knew that when Ruth converted to Judaism, she became as Jewish as anyone born a Jew. God blessed their marriage, as the scroll tells us. And all Israel learned this lesson, too. Not only did Ruth's family include David and Solomon, but in the End of Time, it will also include the Messiah.

[Sources: I Samuel 17:12-13; I Kings 2:4,12]

59

DO YOU KNOW WHY?

1. Why did Naomi return to Israel?

_____

_____

2. Why did Ruth glean in the fields?

_____

_____

3. Why did Boaz invite Ruth to share his food?

_____

_____

4. Why did Boaz tell his workers to let some grain slip from their hands?

_____

_____

5. Why did Boaz go to the city gate?

_____

_____

Choose the Best

Circle the words that
best complete the sentence.

1 **Boaz was**
a poor man.
Naomi's relative.
a gleaner in the fields.

2 **When Naomi returned to Israel**
Elimelech went with her.
her sons died.
it was the time of the harvest.

3 **When Boaz spoke to Naomi's closest relative**
he brought him food.
he gave his robe to Boaz.
he refused to marry Ruth.

4 **Letting people glean in the fields was**
a way of giving _tzedakah_.
forbidden by Jewish law.
a good idea, but very messy.

5 **Ruth said to Naomi, "Do not ask me**
to go to work for you."
to find you a new home."
to leave you."

Who Said It?

THE WOMEN

NAOMI'S CLOSEST RELATIVE

RUTH

BOAZ

ORPAH AND RUTH

NAOMI

NAME SCRAMBLE

Unscramble the letters to see the names of people you have read about.

ELMICELHE _____

ANIMO _____

PORHA _____

TURH _____

ZAOB _____

ESESJ _____

DOBE _____

VDADI _____

WHAT HAPPENED WHEN?

What happened when Naomi decided to return to Israel?

_____

What happened when Ruth went to glean in the fields?

_____

What happened when Boaz woke up at midnight?

_____

What happened when Boaz went to the city gate?

_____

THE PEOPLE AT THE GATE

1. "Let us go with you, to your people," said
_____

2. "Your people shall be my people," said
_____

3. "My daughter, you need a home," said
_____

4. "In that case, I cannot buy it," said
_____

5. "I will marry Ruth and give her children," said
_____

6. "May God make your wife like Rachel and Leah," said
_____

7. "May your grandchild bring you pleasure," said
_____

First Samuel 1-15 שְׁמוּאֵל א

Chapter 8

SAMUEL AND SAUL

nce there was a woman named Hannah who had no children. Each year Hannah went to the Tabernacle at Shiloh to pray. "O God," she said, "give me a child and I will let him serve You all the days of his life." And, in time, God gave a son to Hannah and her husband Elkanah. Hannah named the baby Samuel.

When Samuel was still quite young, Hannah brought him to Shiloh, to Eli the priest. "As long as Samuel lives, he shall serve God," she said. So Samuel lived at the Tabernacle and Eli became his teacher.

In those days there were few prophets. God's word was seldom heard in Israel.

One night, as Eli and Samuel were trying to fall asleep, God called Samuel. "Here I am!" Samuel answered, and he ran to where Eli was sleeping. "I am here," Samuel said.

Eli said, "I did not call. Go back to bed." And Samuel did.

Then God called a second time: "Samuel!" Samuel ran to Eli again, and said, "Here I am. Why do you call me?" And Eli answered, "I did not call, my son. Please, go and lie down."

But God called Samuel a third time. Once again, Samuel ran to Eli, saying, "Here I am. For you *did* call me." Then Eli knew that God was calling Samuel. Eli said, "Go, lie down. If God calls again, you must say, 'Speak to me, O God, I am Your servant who listens.'" So Samuel went back to lie down.

Soon God called as before, "Samuel! Samuel!" And Samuel answered, "Speak, for Your servant listens." From that day on, God was with Samuel. Soon all Israel knew that Samuel was God's prophet. Every year, Samuel traveled throughout the land–from one holy place to another–judging the people in each place. In this way, Samuel judged Israel as long as he lived.

When Samuel was old he appointed his sons to be judges over Israel. But his sons took bribes and they judged unfairly. In time, the leaders of Israel's tribes gathered together and came to see Samuel. They said, "You are old, and your sons do not walk in your ways. Choose a king to judge us so that we may be like all the other nations."

Samuel did not like this idea. But God said to Samuel, "Hear what the people are saying to you. They have not lost their faith in you. They have lost their faith in Me, saying that God should not be King any more! Do as they say, but first warn them about kings."

Samuel spoke God's words to the people. "A king will take your sons to drive his chariots and ride his horses. He will take your sons to serve in his army and to plow his fields. A king will take your daughters to be maids in his palace. He will take your best fields, vineyards, and olive groves. And a king will force you to pay taxes. You will be his servants.

Then you will cry out, 'Why did we choose a king?" But God will pay no attention to your cries."

Nevertheless, the people insisted, "Give us a king and make us like other nations. Let our king judge us and fight our battles." And Samuel paid attention to them and repeated their words to God. God said, "Do as they say. Give them a king." And Samuel sent the people back to their cities.

Among the tribe of Benjamin lived a young man named Saul. In all Israel, he was the tallest, most handsome man. God whispered in Samuel's ear, "Tomorrow I will send you a man from the tribe of Benjamin. You shall anoint him king over My people Israel. And he shall save My people from their enemy, the Philistines."

When Saul appeared, Samuel took a small jar of oil and poured it on

his head. Samuel kissed Saul and said, "God has chosen you to be king of Israel."

Then Samuel called the Israelites together and announced that Saul was their king. But when they turned to see their new king, he could not be found. They asked, "Where is this man?" And God answered, "There he is, hiding." So the people ran and brought him out. And when he stood, they saw that he towered over them, head and shoulders. And Samuel said, "See the one God has chosen! There is no one else like him." Then all the people shouted, "Long live the king!"

Samuel explained to the people how kings and queens behave, and he wrote all this in a book and stored it in the Ark. And Samuel sent the people home. Saul, too, started for home. But God touched the hearts of many brave Israelites and they went with Saul.

Two years passed. Saul trained three thousand of the men with him to be soldiers. And one thousand Israelites attacked a troop of Philistines. Then all the Philistines swore revenge. Samuel told Saul, "Gather the soldiers for war, but do not go to battle until I return to make a sacrifice to God."

"Sound the *shofar* throughout the land!" Saul ordered. And the Israelites came to join Saul's army. But, day after day, Saul waited for Samuel.

Meanwhile, the Philistine army gathered. There were so many Philistines that the Israelites grew frightened. The people began to run away from Saul's camp. They ran to hide in caves, behind thorn bushes and rocks, in holes, and in wells.

When Saul saw his people scattering, he was afraid to wait for Samuel any longer. So Saul himself offered the sacrifice to God, praying for victory. Just then, Samuel arrived. Saul went out to greet him.

Samuel was angry. "What have you done? You disobeyed God by not waiting. Now God will find a new king, one who will listen to God's commands." Samuel was sad for Saul, but he never came to Saul again. And God was unhappy for making Saul king over Israel.

Even so, God gave Saul a victory against the Philistines that day. And Saul ruled over Israel, fighting against Israel's enemies on every side. All the days of Saul were days of war.

This stand found at Shiloh was used for burning incense, a mixture of herbs, gums, and tree resins that produces a pleasant aroma.

WHAT DOES IT MEAN?
"There is no one else like him."

When Samuel said that there was no one else like Saul, he meant that no one else was as tall or handsome as Saul. He did not mean that Saul was braver than other people in Israel, or even stronger. In fact, Saul was very brave and very strong, but never very sure of himself. He always wondered if he deserved to be king.

Part of growing up is learning to be sure of yourself. The Bible says that when King Saul began ruling, he was like a one year old child. When he was made king, he hid because he was afraid that the people might not like him. As time went on, he learned that people like you for what you do, not for who you are. No matter who you are, if you do bad things people will turn against you; and if you do good things people will learn to love you.

WHAT DOES IT TEACH?
Samuel the Prophet

Our teachers say: Samuel was just thirteen years old when he heard God's call. Thirteen is a joyful age in Judaism. It is the age of *Bar* and *Bat Mitzvah.*

There was no *Bar* or *Bat Mitzvah* ceremony in the days of Samuel. The ceremony is not the most important thing, even now. *Bar* means

"son" and *Bat* means "daughter." *Bar* or *Bat Mitzvah* means "child of the commandments" or "a person born to keep the commandments." Up to age thirteen, you are your parents' responsibility. When you reach the age of *Bar* or *Bat Mitzvah,* you are responsible for your own actions. You must choose to walk in God's way—to be "a person born to keep the commandments."

67

The high place called Shiloh, where Samuel heard God's call.

A LESSON FROM THE PROPHETS

How David
Became King

God said to Samuel, "I have taken away Saul's kingdom. Go to Bethlehem for I have chosen one of Jesse's sons to be king." Samuel said, "If Saul hears that I am going to appoint a new king, he will kill me."

"Say you are going to Bethlehem to make a sacrifice," said God.

Samuel went to Bethlehem. He said, "I have come to offer a sacrifice to God." And he invited Jesse and his sons to the sacrifice. Then Samuel looked at Jesse's sons. He walked toward the tallest and most handsome of them. But God said, "Pay no attention to this one. Remember, people do not see the way God sees! People see only what a person looks like, but God sees into the heart." Then Samuel walked toward each of the other sons. But God had not chosen any of them. Samuel said to Jesse, "Have you any other sons?" And Jesse said, "David, my youngest son, is out tending the sheep."

Samuel said, "Send for your youngest son." And, when David appeared, God said, "Anoint this one king, for David is the one I have chosen."

[Source: I Samuel 16:1-13]

Above: A horn decorated with gold bands. It was used to hold oil for anointing. *Right:* A third-century Jewish artist painted this picture of Samuel anointing David.

BOAZ

MANOAH

NAOMI

SAUL

HANNAH

Who Are They?

• Naomi's relative •
• Samson's father •
• Priest at Shiloh •
• Moses' brother •
• Ruth's mother-in-law •
• Hannah's husband •
• Samuel's mother •
• God's prophet •
• King of Israel •
• A Judge •

ELI

SAMUEL

ELKANAH

DEBORAH

AARON

69

REBUS

The ☉-s of Sa-🐴 were 2 Sa-🐴 U R old & your ways. Choose a 👑

WHAT IS TRUE?

Mark the true statements with a "T" and put an "F" before the false ones.

☐ 1. Hannah prayed to God for a child.

☐ 2. Samuel had two brothers.

☐ 3. Hannah brought Samuel to the Tabernacle to serve God.

☐ 4. Saul was Samuel's teacher.

☐ 5. Samuel's sons were great judges.

☐ 6. The people wanted to be like the other nations and have a king.

☐ 7. Samuel ran to Eli and said, "I hear God calling me."

☐ 8. David was Jesse's youngest son.

☐ 9. Saul never offered a sacrifice to God.

☐ 10. God chose Eli to be king of Israel.

WHY? BECAUSE…

1. Hannah brought Samuel to the Tabernacle at Shiloh because

2. All Israel knew that Samuel was God's prophet because

3. The people asked for a king because

4. Samuel poured oil on Saul's head because

5. Saul did not wait for Samuel to offer the sacrifice because

6. God was unhappy for making Saul king because

You Be the Teacher

Choose one of the lessons and explain what it means in your own words.

■ People like you for what you do, not for who you are.

■ When you reach the age of *Bar* or *Bat Mitzvah*, you are responsible for your own actions.

■ People see only what a person looks like, but God sees into a person's heart.

good judges. The [pea]-ple said your [sun]-s do [knot] walk in 2 judge us & fight our [bat]-tles."

WORD SEARCH

Look across and down to find 12 hidden words. Use the words to complete the sentences.

```
T  A  B  E  R  N  A  C  L  E
E  S  O  L  D  I  E  R  S  C
A  P  R  O  P  H  E  T  D  K
C  W  A  I  T  W  A  R  A  I
H  D  E  L  M  L  D  I  Y  N
E  J  U  D  G  E  S  B  S  G
R  B  W  I  S  R  A  E  L  V
```

1. Samuel lived at the _____ at Shiloh.
2. Eli was his _____.
3. Samuel was God's _____.
4. Samuel's sons were unfair _____.
5. Saul lived among the _____ of Benjamin.
6. Saul was chosen to be _____ of _____.
7. Samuel poured _____ on Saul's head.
8. Saul trained the men to be _____.
9. Saul did not _____ for Samuel to make a sacrifice.
10. All the _____ of Saul were days of _____.

71

Chapter 9

DAVID IN THE DAYS OF SAUL

he Philistines camped on a mountain, and Israel camped on a mountain across from them, so that the valley was between them. Then the Philistines sent out their hero, Goliath of Gat. He was a gigantic man. He wore bronze armor from head to foot. Another man went out with him, just to carry his heavy bronze shield.

"Why should we go to war?" Goliath shouted to the Israelites. "Choose one man to fight for Israel. If he kills me, all Philistines will be your servants. But if I kill him, then all Israelites will serve us." Saul and the soldiers of Israel heard Goliath's words and they trembled. And Goliath came out morning and evening, every day for forty days.

Now David's three oldest brothers were with Saul. David's father said, "Take food to your brothers. Then bring back news of them."

Early in the morning, David took the food and went to his brothers. As he was talking to them, Goliath came out to challenge Israel once again. And David heard Goliath's words. The men of Israel shivered in

fear. They asked David, "Have you seen this giant man, Goliath? Saul will reward any Israelite who kills him, but we are all frightened." David asked, "Why do you let this Philistine challenge the armies of the living God?"

When Saul heard David's words, he said, "Bring the man to me." Then David said to Saul, "Do not fret. I will go and fight this Philistine."

"You are too young," said Saul.

But David said, "I am a shepherd. When a wild beast comes to kill a lamb, I attack it. And if it rises to kill me, I catch it by its beard and kill it. I have killed both lion and bear; and this Philistine will be like one of them. God saved me from the paw of the lion and God will save me from the hand of Goliath." Then Saul said, "Go, and may God be with you!"

David wore no armor and carried no shield. He carried only his shepherd's staff and his sling. He found five smooth stones in the brook and put them in his shepherd's pouch. And he walked out to meet Goliath.

When Goliath looked down and saw David, he began to laugh. "Am I a dog?" he asked. "Do you want me to play with your stick? Come close. I will feed your dead body to the birds!"

Then David said, "You have heavy armor, but I am protected by the God of Israel. God needs neither sword nor spear. With God's help, I will kill you."

As Goliath came closer, David took a stone from his pouch. He placed it in his slingshot, whirled the slingshot, and threw the stone. The stone struck Goliath's forehead hard and sank deep into his flesh. With a mighty thud, Goliath fell to the earth. Then David took Goliath's sword and killed Goliath.

When the Philistines saw their champion fall, they ran away. And the army of Israel ran after them, shouting cries of war, wounding many.

That day, Saul said to David, "From now on, you will stay with me." And Jonathan, the son of Saul, became David's best friend. Jonathan felt even closer to David than to his own soul. Jonathan and David made a covenant to always love and help one another. And, as a sign, Jonathan gave

David his robe, his armor, his sword, his bow, and his belt—the clothing of a prince.

David and Saul walked side by side. In every city, women with musical instruments came out singing and dancing in joy. The women sang,

Saul has slain his thousands,
But David has killed tens of thousands.

The women's song made Saul very angry. "They speak of David's ten thousands, and of me they say only thousands," he thought. "Perhaps they also want David as their king?" And Saul was jealous of David from that day on.

The very next day, David was playing on the lyre when an evil spirit gripped Saul. The king raved and raged in his house, waving his spear in his hand. Then Saul threw the spear at David, trying to pin him to the wall. But David moved quickly, and the spear missed twice. So Saul was afraid of David–for God was with David and not with Saul.

Saul sent David away to be a captain in the army. David was a good leader, and God was with him. All Israel and Judah loved David. Even Michal, Saul's daughter, loved David–and that made Saul even more afraid. When he tried once again to kill David, David ran away.

David asked Jonathan, "Why does your father wish to kill me?"

But Jonathan said, "If I knew that my father wished you dead, would I not tell you? I will go and ask. You do as I say: Return here on the third day, and wait. I will shoot three arrows, and I will send a boy after them. If I say to the boy, 'Look close for the arrows'–then, all is well. But if I say to the boy, 'Look, the arrows are far off'–then you must run for your life." So David hid in the field and waited.

When Jonathan spoke to Saul, the king said, "Do you not understand? As long as David lives, you shall never be king. Bring David to me. He must die." And Jonathan said, "Why should he be killed? What has he done?" And Saul answered by throwing his spear in anger.

In the morning, Jonathan went out into the field, taking a boy with him. He said to this servant, "Run after the arrows I shoot." And he shot an arrow far past the boy, crying, "The arrow is far off. Hurry. Do not hesitate." And, all along, he was really talking to David who was hiding.

Jonathan gave his bow and arrow to the boy and sent him away. And, when the boy was gone, David came out of hiding. Then David and Jonathan kissed one another, weeping together.

Jonathan said to David, "Go in peace, for we made a covenant before God to love one another forever." So David ran away, and Jonathan returned to his father.

WHAT DOES IT MEAN?

Jonathan and David made a covenant...

The love of best friends is blessed by God in the story of David and Jonathan. Their promise to love one another is called a "covenant." The Hebrew word is *brit*. The Bible uses the same word for the covenants God made with Noah, Abraham, Isaac, Jacob, and all Israel.

Jonathan saved David's life, knowing all along that David would be king instead of him. That is the special secret of friendship: Your best friend is the one who *always* helps you. And the Bible seems to be teaching

One part of the mosaic floor from the sixth-century synagogue of Bet Alpha shows the sign of the Archer. The bow and arrow was a common weapon in the time of David and Jonathan.

that when you make a promise to be someone's best friend, it is a holy promise—like a covenant made with God.

WHAT DOES IT TEACH?

Small and Large

Goliath was huge, a champion among soldiers. Saul's whole army was afraid of him. But small David was not afraid. David had faith. David believed that God would help him. When Goliath teased him, David answered, "God needs neither sword nor spear."

God is not always on the side of the small and weak just as God is not always on the side of the strong. But one thing is certain: It is God who decides who will win the battle. God helped Joshua, Deborah, and Gideon —and even Samson. David hoped God would protect him, too. Not because David was small, but because Goliath believed that he was greater than God.

A stone carving shows a man using a slingshot like the one David used against Goliath.

77

The Philistines were enemies of Israel and of Egypt. This Egyptian wall carving shows Philistine soldiers captured in battle.

A LESSON FROM THE PROPHETS

David Saves Saul's Life

Saul took three thousand soldiers to find David and kill him. He heard that David was hiding in caves in the hills near Ein Gedi. But the caves were deep, and finding David was difficult. One hot day, Saul went into a cave to rest. He did not know that David was inside that very cave.

David crept silently to where Saul was sleeping. He used his sword to cut a small piece from Saul's robe. A short while later, Saul woke up and left the cave. But David called after him. "My lord, Saul," David said. And Saul turned, surprised to see David behind him.

David held the piece of robe in his hand. "I had the power to kill you today. But I do not wish to hurt you. Why, then, do you wish to hurt me?" Saul saw the piece of robe and knew it was his, and he began to cry.

"Why do you cry?" David asked. And Saul answered, "I cry because you are a better person than I am. The kingdom will soon be yours. For you have done good for me, though I wished only to do evil to you." Then Saul said, "Promise you will not kill me or Jonathan, and I will never again try to kill you." David promised. And Saul and his soldiers returned home.

[Source: II Samuel 24:1-23]

1
The Philistine hero was
  a huge sandwich.
  a giant named Goliath.
  a fat man named Gat.

2
The soldiers of Saul were
  frightened of the Philistine hero.
  unhappy to see David.
  ready to fight lions and bears.

3
Saul said that David was
  the biggest coward in the world.
  too old to go into battle.
  too young to fight.

4
David wore no armor, but he
  was wearing sandals and stockings.
  carried a bear in one hand and a lion in the other.
  carried five smooth stones.

5
The giant laughed at David and said,
  "I will feed your dead body to the birds."
  "You are too big to fight with me."
  "We can make peace."

6
David and Jonathan promised
  to go to the Tabernacle together.
  to be good sons to Saul.
  to be friends always.

7
As David and Saul passed by, the women of the cities
  came out to sing and dance for them.
  gave them bread and wine.
  laughed at them.

8
Saul tried to kill David with his
  slingshot.
  lyre.
  spear.

9
Jonathan told David to run away if
  Jonathan shot ten arrows in the air.
  Jonathan told the boy to look far off for the arrows.
  Jonathan could not find the arrows he shot.

10
Jonathan shot three arrows and told the boy
  to run away before the arrows hit him.
  to leave the arrows and go back home.
  to look far off for the arrows.

LOOKING FOR UNDERSTANDING

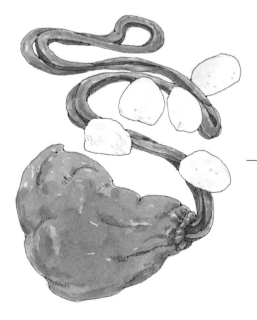

79

DOT TO DOT

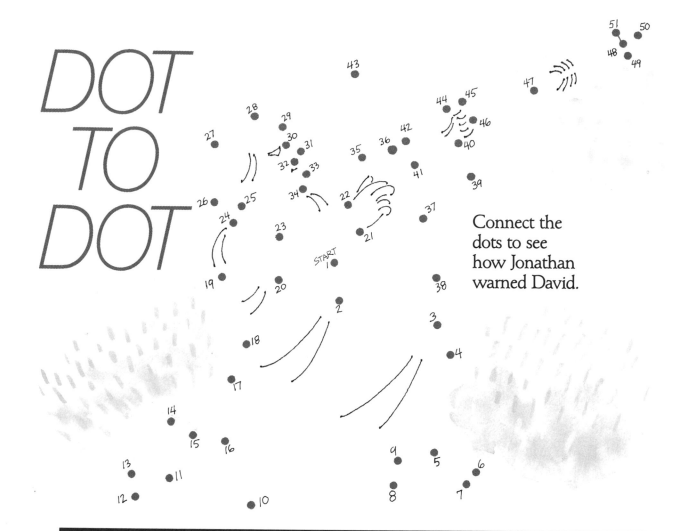

Connect the dots to see how Jonathan warned David.

FRIENDSHIP

Jonathan and David were best friends. Circle the words that describe Jonathan. The words that are left will describe another person. Who is it?

_____.

LOYAL

JEALOUS

FAITHFUL

LOVING

AFRAID

KIND

HELPFUL

MAD

WORRIED

GENTLE

HONEST

GOOD

ANGRY

ENVIOUS

BITTER

GENEROUS

SCARED

COMPLETE THE STORY

The Philistine hero Goliath was as tall as a _____.
He challenged the Israelites to choose one man to
_____ him. David placed a stone in his
_____. It struck Goliath's _____.
Then David killed Goliath with his own
_____. Jonathan was Saul's _____.
When Saul tried to _____ David,
David _____ away.

QUESTIONS TO ANSWER

1. Why did David go to see his brothers?

2. Why was David not afraid to fight Goliath?

3. Why did Saul become angry with David?

4. How did the war between David and Saul end?

5. Why did David cut a piece of Saul's robe?

6. Why did Jonathan help David to escape from Saul?

7. Why did the women dance and sing?

8. Why did the Philistines run away?

81

Second Samuel 6-12 שְׁמוּאֵל ב

First Kings 2 מְלָכִים א

Chapter 10

DAVID AND BATHSHEBA

ing David built a palace in Jerusalem and brought the Ark of God there. And Jerusalem was called the City of David.

Now the king said to Nathan the prophet, "I live in a lovely house, but God's Ark is still covered by a tent. I will build a wondrous temple for God." Nathan said, "Do that, for God is with you." Yet, that night God said to Nathan, "I made David king, though he was only a shepherd. I made David's name great. In time to come, David's son will be king. Let David's son build a temple for Me, and I will make David's children kings forever." And Nathan spoke these words and told this vision to David.

Then King David sat before God and said, "There is none like You, O God; and there is no other God besides You. And Your people, Israel, is special in all the earth. You have made Israel Your very own people forever and You are their God."

It happened in the spring, the time of the year when kings lead their armies to battle. King David sent his army out, but he stayed in Jerusalem.

83

Late one afternoon, David went for a stroll on the roof of his royal palace. From the roof he saw a woman bathing. And the woman was very beautiful. David sent a servant to ask who the woman was. And the servant reported, "She is Bathsheba, the wife of Uriah who is away in your army."

David sent for Bathsheba and she stayed with him awhile before returning home. Later, she sent a message to the king, saying, "You and I will soon have a child."

So David sent for Uriah. And when Uriah came before him, David asked how the army was doing. Then David said to Uriah, "Go home." So Uriah left and the king sent him gifts of food. But Uriah did not go to his house. He slept at the gate of the palace, with the soldiers of the king. In the morning, David sent for Uriah again. "Why did you not go home?" the king asked.

And Uriah said, "Your soldiers are living in tents far away. I wanted to be like them so that when I return they will not be jealous of me."

Then David wrote a letter to his general and told Uriah to deliver it. The letter said: "Put Uriah at the front of the hottest battle, and make certain that he is killed." So it happened, and so Uriah died.

When Bathsheba heard that Uriah her husband was dead, she mourned for him. And when her mourning was over, David sent for Bathsheba and Bathsheba became his wife and gave birth to his son. But God was not pleased by the thing David had done.

God sent Nathan the prophet to David. Nathan told David this story:

> A rich man and a poor one lived in the same city. The rich man had many flocks and herds. The poor man had only one little lamb that he loved like his own child. A guest came to the rich man, but he refused to cook a sheep from his own flocks. Instead, he took the poor man's lamb and cooked it for his guest.

When David heard this story, he grew angry. He said to Nathan, "The man who has done this shall be put to death! But, first, he shall give back four lambs for the one he stole. For he had no pity."

Then Nathan said to David, "You are the man! The God of Israel says,

> I saved you from Saul and made you king over Israel. I gave you Saul's house and all of Israel. If that was too little, I would have given you much more! Why then did you break God's commandment? Why did you murder Uriah and take his wife to be your wife?
>
> Now your house will know the sword. I will raise up enemies in your own house.

Then David said to Nathan, "I have sinned against God." And Nathan said, "God will punish you, but you shall not die. Yet the child born to you and Bathsheba shall surely die."

After Nathan left, God brought an illness on the child. David fasted. He prayed for the life of his child. He would not rise from the ground. But on the seventh day, the child died. And David's servants were afraid. They said, "We spoke to him when the child was alive, but he would not listen to us. He would not eat. He would not rise from the floor. Now the child is dead. Perhaps he will do worse to himself if he knows it."

But David saw his servants whispering, and he knew that the child was dead. So David asked, "Is the child dead?" And they answered, "Yes, he is dead."

Then David rose from the ground, washed, and changed his clothes. He prayed. Then he came home and ate. His servants asked, "What are you doing? You fasted and wept for the child while he lived, but now that the child is dead, you rise and eat." David answered, "I fasted and wept in the hope that God might still save the child. But now all my fasting and weeping cannot bring back my son."

Then David comforted Bathsheba. And, in time, she had another son, and David called his name Solomon. And God loved Solomon.

Years passed. David's days were almost at an end. He called Solomon and said, "Soon I must die. Be strong. If you walk in God's ways and keep God's commandments, God will guard over the House of David forever, and one of our children will always be on the throne of Israel."

And Jerusalem was called the City of David.

Saul and Jonathan died in a battle against the Philistines. "And the leaders of Judah [in the south] came and anointed David king of Judah." Meanwhile, the tribes of the north called themselves "Israel" and anointed a son of Saul to be their king. So the land was divided into two kingdoms—Judah and Israel—and there was war between them. But David grew stronger from year to year and the Israelites grew weaker. Finally, the king of Israel was murdered by two of his own followers. "Then the leaders of Israel came to David…and they anointed David king over Israel." This ended the war between the tribes of the north and the tribes of the south.

David captured Zion, the city of the Jebusites, which was also called Jerusalem. "And David called it the City of David." Our teachers say that the word *Jerusalem* means "city of peace." Jerusalem lay between the tribes of Israel and the tribes of Judah, and it belonged to neither of them. And it was high in the hills, a place that could be protected easily. David wisely chose this city to be his capital. He made it a sign of peace between north and south.

A Jewish artist carved the Ark of the Covenant mounted on wheels some time between 200 and 300 C.E., long after the Ark had disappeared.

In the time of King David, the city of Jerusalem was mainly in this valley below where the city walls stand today.

A Phoenician statuette of a woman bathing reminds us of the story of David and Bathsheba.

WHAT DOES IT TEACH?

David and Nathan

In ancient times, kings could do anything they pleased. If a king saw something he wanted, he just took it. This was not the way of the kings of Israel. They followed the same commandments as the people did. But David forgot this when he stole Bathsheba from her husband Uriah. And he forgot it when he sent Uriah into battle to be killed. His friend, Nathan the prophet, told the story of the lamb to remind him.

Other ancient kings would have laughed and ordered Nathan put to death. Not David. He knew that he had done wrong, and he prayed to be forgiven. He never again slipped into the ways of foreign kings. He studied Torah constantly.

A LESSON FROM THE WRITINGS

David—The Sweet Singer of Israel

David loved music. He practiced playing the lyre, a small harp. And he invented other musical instruments.

He taught the servants of the priests to sing God's praises. And our teachers say that he wrote most of the Book of Psalms, a book made up of songs to praise God. David's favorite psalms were those that begin with the word *ashray*, "Happy is the person..." Here is a song of David:

> How good it is and how pleasant
>   When people live side by side.
> It is like perfumed oil on the head
>   running down into the beard of
>   Aaron,
>   that falls over the collar of his
>   robe;
>   like the dew on the high
>   mountain
>   that falls on the mountains of
>   Zion.
> For God commands blessing there,
>   life that flows on forever.

[Sources: Berachot 9a-10b; Psalm 133]

The lyre David played was very much like the one held by this ancient clay figure.

87

Help
King David
bring the Ark
to Jerusalem.

MAZE

WHAT HAPPENED WHERE?

Complete each sentence with the correct place. Look back in your book to find the answers when you do not remember.

JERUSALEM   MOUNT NEBO   EIN GEDI   BETHLEHEM   SHILOH
EIN HAROD   GAZA   JERICHO   MOUNT TABOR

1. Moses died on_____.
2. David built a palace in_____.
3. Hannah prayed for a child at_____.
4. Ruth and Boaz met in_____.
5. David hid in a cave near_____.
6. Samson was put into prison in_____.
7. Gideon and his followers camped in_____.
8. Joshua won a great battle at_____.
9. Barak fought against Sisera on_____.

BROKEN COMMANDMENTS

Read the Ten Commandments in Chapter 2. Which commandments did King David break? Explain your answer.

MISSING LETTERS

Here are eight words that you know. Fill in the missing letters. Then read down to see what God said to Nathan the prophet.

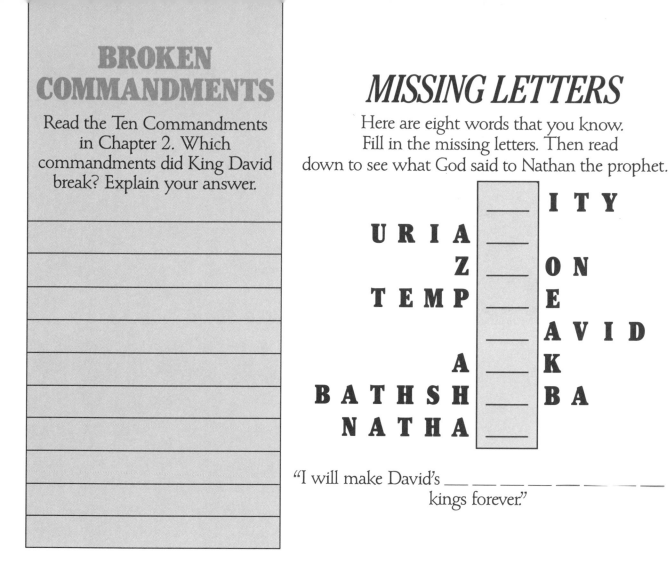

		___	I T Y	
U R I A		___		
	Z	___	O N	
T E M P		___	E	
		___	A V I D	
	A	___	K	
B A T H S H		___	B A	
N A T H A		___		

"I will make David's __ __ __ __ __ __ __ __
kings forever."

TRUE OR FALSE?

Put a "T" beside each true statement. Put an "F" beside each statement that is not true.

1. David brought the Ark of the Covenant to Jerusalem.
2. Nathan told David not to build the Temple.
3. David saw Bathsheba while he was walking by her house.
4. David told his general to put Uriah at the front of the battle.
5. Nathan told David a story that made David very angry.
6. David commanded that Nathan should be put to death.
7. David fasted and prayed for the life of his child.
8. David married Bathsheba after Uriah died.
9. Saul and Jonathan died when they caught a terrible disease.
10. Jerusalem was also called "Zion" and "The City of David."

89

First Kings 3-8 מְלָכִים א

Chapter 11

KING SOLOMON JUDGES

ow Solomon made a peace treaty with Pharaoh, King of Egypt, and married Pharaoh's daughter. He brought her to the City of David while he was still building the Temple, his royal palace, and the wall around Jerusalem. And God appeared to Solomon in a dream, saying, "Ask for anything! What shall I give you?"

Solomon said: "O God, You have made me king in the place of my father David. But I know so very little. Give me an understanding heart and teach me to know good from evil so that I can judge this great people of Yours."

And God was pleased. "You ask for wisdom, and not for long life or riches. You ask for understanding, and not for the death of your enemies.

I will give you a wise and understanding heart. And I will also give you riches and honor. You shall be the greatest of kings. And, if you walk in My ways, as your father David did, then I will give you long life, too."

Solomon awoke and knew that it had been a dream. But he stood before the Ark of the Covenant and thanked God.

Two women came to stand before Solomon in judgment. One said, "O King, we two women live together in one house. I gave birth to a child and three days later, she also gave birth. And there were only the two of us in the house, no one else. In the night, her baby died. She waited until I was sleeping. Then she took my baby and put her dead baby near me. When I awoke in the morning, I saw the dead baby, but he was not my child."

The other woman said, "No! The living one is my baby, and the dead one was yours!" And the first woman said, "No! The dead one is your baby, and the living one is mine."

Then the king said, "This is my judgment: Bring a sword and divide the living child in two. Give half to one woman, and half to the other."

Then the real mother spoke to the king, for she loved her baby and did not want it to die. She said, "O King, do not kill the baby! Give her the living child." But the other woman said, "No. Let the baby be divided."

So the king said, "Give the baby to the first woman. She is his mother."

And when the people of Israel heard of Solomon's judgment, they saw that God had truly given him wisdom.

Solomon ruled over all the kingdoms from the river in the north as far as Egypt in the south. They served Solomon all the days of his life. He was the wisest man who lived. He was famous throughout the world. He spoke three thousand proverbs, and wrote one thousand and five poems. He was wise in the ways of trees, of animals, of birds, of insects, and of fish. And people were sent by all the kings of the earth to hear Solomon's wisdom.

It took Solomon seven years to complete the building of the Temple.

The time came to bring the Ark of the Covenant into the Temple. Solomon called all the leaders of the people to come to Jerusalem. Then the priests brought the Ark, the Tabernacle, and all the holy things used to serve God. The priests placed the Ark in the Holy of Holies – the small, center room of the Temple. And when the priests came out of the Holy of Holies, a cloud rose inside and God's glory filled the Temple.

Solomon announced, "God said, 'I will live in the dark cloud.'" Everyone stood, and the king prayed for the whole congregation. He said: "Blessed be God, who spoke to my father David. My father planned to build this Temple. But God said, 'Let your son build My house.' So I have built the Temple for God."

When Solomon finished praying, he raised his hands to heaven. Then he raised his voice and blessed all the congregation of Israel, saying:

> May God be with us now, as God was with our ancestors. And let your heart be filled with God, so that you will walk in God's ways and keep the commandments.

In this way, Solomon and all the children of Israel dedicated the Temple as the house of God.

A modern model of the Temple Solomon built in Jerusalem.

WHAT DOES IT MEAN?

...God had truly given him wisdom.

Many legends grew up around Solomon's wisdom. It was said that he could speak with birds, beasts, fish, and plants. Here is one legend:

> The Temple was a symbol of peace, even as Jerusalem was "the city of peace." Metal could not be used to cut the stones for the Temple because tools of war are made of metal. But Solomon spoke to the animals and they told him about the *shamir* worm. The *shamir* could shape the hardest rock—even diamonds. The *shamir* was kept in Paradise from the sixth day of Creation until the day Solomon needed it. Solomon sent an eagle to fetch it. It was the *shamir* that carved out the stones of the Temple, and shaped the stone of the great altar. When the Temple was complete, Solomon returned the *shamir* to its home. Later, when the Temple was destroyed the *shamir* vanished.

Jews remember the Temple as they pray at the Western Wall in Jerusalem. The Western Wall is the last standing piece of the outer walls of the Second Temple.

93

To build the Temple, Solomon brought huge cedar logs from Phoenicia. The logs in this carving are being transported by sea.

Solomon the Writer

Our sages said: Solomon wrote three books of the Bible—the Book of Proverbs, the Song of Songs, and Ecclesiastes. The Book of Proverbs is made up of sayings of wisdom. The Song of Songs is a poem of love. And Ecclesiastes is a sermon on the meaning of life. All of them are found in the section of the Bible called The Writings, but they are very different from one another. The sages asked: How could one person write three books that are so different?

Rabbi Yohanan explained: Solomon wrote the Song of Songs when he was young and his heart filled with the joys of love. In his middle age, he wrote the Book of Proverbs which explains the best way to live a good life. And he waited until he grew old to write the Book of Ecclesiastes which tells how short life is and how difficult. To really understand Solomon's wisdom, we need all three of his writings.

94

Lessons from The Book of Proverbs

Solomon said that his Book of Proverbs was written so that "the wise may hear, and grow wiser." These are some of his proverbs:

The ways of wisdom are ways of pleasantness
    And all its paths are peace.
Walk with the wise and you shall be wise;
    Be a friend to fools and you will suffer.
A wise son makes a glad father.

Iron sharpens iron—
    One who is wise makes friends wiser.
Pride goes before destruction,
    Stubbornness goes before a fall.
Without wood, the fire goes out,
    Without someone to gossip, the rumors stop.
Train up a child in the way he should go,
    And even when he is old, he will not depart from it.

[Source: Proverbs]

Farming and orchard-keeping is hard work. Proverbs says: "The lazy one who does not plow before winter, will beg during the harvest and have nothing."

CHOOSE THE BEST

Circle the words that best complete the sentence.

1. Solomon asked God for wisdom and understanding because he wanted to
    marry Pharaoh's daughter.
    know good from evil and judge the people fairly.
    build a great palace for his wives.

2. When the sword was brought in, the child's real mother
    prayed in the Temple.
    let the baby be divided.
    begged to give her child to the other woman.

3. Solomon was wise in the ways of
    cooking chickens and beef.
    trees, animals, birds, and fish.
    cutting stone.

4. The priests placed the Ark of the Covenant
    under Deborah's palm tree.
    in a big tent called the Tabernacle.
    in a room called the Holy of Holies.

5. When the Temple was finished, Solomon
    blessed all the congregation of Israel.
    followed King David to the Palace.
    took a long vacation.

YOU BE THE TEACHER

Choose a proverb in the chapter and write it in your own words.

_____

_____

_____

_____

_____

_____

_____

MYSTERY WORD

Cross out any letter that appears two times.
Write the remaining letters to complete the sentence.

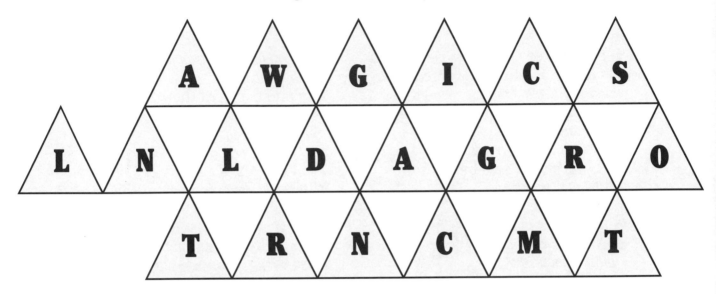

King Solomon asked for ___ ___ ___ ___ ___ ___.

WHAT IS MOST IMPORTANT?

All of the things on this list are important. What is most important to you? Place a number next to each thing, with 1 for the most important and 7 for the least important.

_____ GOOD HEALTH
_____ POPULARITY
_____ INTELLIGENCE
_____ SUCCESS
_____ WEALTH
_____ FAMILY
_____ FRIENDS

MAKE A WISH

If you were granted one wish, what would that wish be, and why?

I would choose _____

_____

_____

because _____

_____

_____

_____

IDEA SCRAMBLE

Put each set of words in the correct order to see part of a proverb.

SON MAKES WISE A FATHER A GLAD

_____

WITHOUT TO RUMORS SOMEONE GOSSIP STOP

_____

ONE WISE WHO WISER MAKES IS FRIENDS

_____

GO THE TRAIN IN WAY UP CHILD A SHOULD HE

_____

97

Chapter 12

ELIJAH AND THE PRIESTS OF BAAL

n time, a man named Ahab became the king of Israel. He married a foreign princess named Jezebel who came from the land of Sidon. Jezebel brought four hundred and fifty prophets of her god Baal into Israel, and many idols besides.

When God saw that the people were worshipping idols, God sent a prophet from the region of Gilead. His name was Elijah the Tishbite.

Elijah said to King Ahab, "I swear by God, no dew or rain shall fall unless I say it can." And no rain fell in Israel. God said to Elijah, "Now you must hide. Go to Wadi Kerit. Drink from the brook. I will send ravens to feed you."

Elijah did as God said. He stayed near Wadi Kerit. Morning and evening, ravens brought him bread and meat. And he drank from the brook, until even Wadi Kerit dried up.

Many days passed. At last God said, "I am sending rain. Go and tell Ahab." So Elijah found Ahab. Now, when the king saw Elijah, he said, "Is that you, you troubler of Israel?"

Elijah answered, "I am not troubling Israel, you are! You are the one who forgot God's commandments. You are the one who worships idols!"

And Elijah said, "Bring the four hundred and fifty priests of your idol Baal to Mount Carmel, and tell all Israel to meet us there." And Ahab did this.

On Mount Carmel, Elijah spoke to all the people. "How long will it be before you make up your minds? If God is God, you must obey God's commands and worship God. Otherwise obey the idol Baal." But the people said nothing.

Then Elijah said, "I am God's only prophet. But Baal has four hundred and fifty prophets. Now bring two bulls. Let Baal's prophets kill one bull and cut it up as a sacrifice. I will make the other bull ready. But we will put no fire under the animals. Let them pray to their god and I will pray to the One God. The God who sends down fire for the sacrifice is the true God."

Then the priests of Baal prepared a bull and prayed to Baal from morning to noon, saying, "O Baal, hear us!" They danced wildly around their altar. But there was no answer.

At noon, Elijah teased them. "Cry louder," he called. "Perhaps Baal is busy or away from home. Perhaps Baal is sleeping and must be awakened." They cried louder. They slashed themselves with knives and spears until they were covered with blood. But there was no answer.

Then Elijah said to the people, "Come close." He took twelve stones, one for each tribe of Israel, and built an altar for God. Around it, he made a deep trench. He set wood on the altar, cut the bull in pieces, and placed the pieces on the wood. He said, "Pour water on the sacrifice and on the wood." Then he said, "Do it again," and they poured more water on the altar. He said, "Do it a third time," and they did it a third time. Water ran down the altar, even filling the trench all around.

When it was the time of the evening sacrifice, Elijah said, "O God of Abraham, Isaac, and Jacob. Show the people this day that You are God in Israel, and that I have done all this at Your word."

Then fire fell from heaven. The sacrifice was swallowed up in flames. The wood, the stones, the dust, and even the water in the trench—all was aflame. When the people saw this, they fell on their faces, saying, "God alone is God! There is only the One God!"

Then Elijah said to them, "Capture the prophets of Baal! Do not let one escape!" The people captured the prophets of Baal and all were put to death. Elijah said to Ahab, "Now the rains will fall." And the sky grew dark with clouds and wind, and there was a heavy rain.

King Ahab told Jezebel all that Elijah had done. And Jezebel promised to kill Elijah. Elijah was frightened for his life. He ran to the south, to the desert. And he hid himself in a cave near Mount Sinai. God asked, "What are you doing here, Elijah?" Elijah said, "They want to kill me."

God said, "Go stand on the mountain. I will pass before you." And here is how God passed before him: There was a great and mighty wind tearing at the mountains, breaking the rocks in pieces. But God was not in the wind. There came an earthquake. But God was not in the earthquake. After the earthquake, a fire flamed. But God was not in the fire. Then, after the fire, there came a small soft voice. And Elijah knew it was the voice of God.

God said, "Go, and appoint Jehu to be king over Israel. And appoint Elisha to be My next prophet."

Elijah left his cave and found Elisha. The man was plowing with oxen and Elijah passed by him and threw his robe over him. And Elisha left the oxen and ran after Elijah. "Please let me kiss my father and my mother," he said, "then I will follow you." And Elisha followed Elijah, and served him.

There came a time when Elijah was leaving Gilgal. Elijah said to Elisha, "You stay here. God sends me to Beth-El." But Elisha said, "I will not leave you!" So they went together to Beth-El. The young prophets studying in Beth-El came to Elisha. "Do you know that God will take your master from you today?" they asked. And he said, "Yes, I know. Be silent!"

Then Elijah said, "Elisha, stay here, please. God sends me to Jericho." And Elisha said, "I will not leave you!" So they went together to Jericho. The young prophets studying in Jericho came to Elisha. "Do you know that God will take your master from you today?" they asked. And he answered, "Yes, I know. Be silent!"

Elijah said to Elisha, "Stay here. God sends me to the Jordan River." And Elisha answered, "I will not leave you!" So they went together to the river.

Elijah rolled up his robe and used it to strike the water. And the water divided so that they crossed the river on dry ground. Then Elijah said to Elisha, "Tell me what I can do for you before I am taken away." And Elisha said, "Just pray that I will be nearly as good a prophet as you are."

"What you ask is difficult," Elijah said. "If you see me taken away from you, your wish will be granted. If not, you shall not have your wish."

As they walked along, talking, a chariot of fire with horses of fire suddenly appeared and separated them. And Elijah went up to heaven in a whirlwind. And Elisha saw it. "O my father," he cried. "It is the chariot of Israel!" But Elisha never saw Elijah again.

Elisha picked up the robe that Elijah had dropped, and returned to the Jordan River. He struck the water with Elijah's robe. And the water was divided so that Elisha crossed the river on dry ground. When the young prophets in Jericho saw him, they said, "The spirit of Elijah rests on Elisha." And they came out to meet him, and bowed down to him.

The Israelite king Jehu is shown bowing at the feet of a powerful ruler from the north. A few years later, the Ten Tribes of Israel were conquered and disappeared forever.

King Ahab married Jezebel...

Our sages said that Ahab was not very good or very bad. But the Bible said that Ahab was evil in every way. How could both be true? The sages explain that Jezebel made Ahab evil. Jezebel taught Ahab to worship idols, especially the god called Baal. Jezebel brought idol worship to Israel and Ahab helped her.

Most of us are like Ahab. We are not very good or very bad. Whether you do good or bad depends on the friends you choose. You lead your friends, and your friends lead you. Together, you can grow and change. If you choose your friends wisely, you are likely to do what is right.

Israel and Judah

After the days of Solomon, the tribes of Israel separated from the tribes of Judah. There were two kingdoms once again. No king could hold them together as Saul, David, and Solomon had. The kingdom of Israel built a new capital at Samaria. One king followed another—in Israel and in Judah. There was often war between the two kingdoms. In all this confusion, the prophets spoke out.

The prophets kept God's commandments fresh in the minds of the people. They spoke in the north and in the south. They judged the way people behaved. They reminded people to walk in God's ways. And they left us their teachings—books filled with wonder and wisdom.

An ancient portrait of Baal. In his right hand the god holds a bolt of lightning, while above his head he holds a club.

103

Our oldest copies of books of the Bible are scrolls which were found in caves near the Dead Sea. This scroll contains parts of the Book of Isaiah.

A LESSON FROM THE PROPHETS

The Prophet Isaiah

The Book of Isaiah is really two books. Isaiah spoke to the people of Judah as the kindgom of Israel was being destroyed by the Assyrians. Life in Judah was good—farms were rich, the treasury was full. But the poor were suffering. The people of Judah worshipped idols. And the sacrifices at the Temple were wasteful. He spoke out against these things, promising that God would one day rule over all the world, and there would be peace.

In the days to come, the Temple mount

Will stand firm above the mountains and tower above the hills.

All nations will gaze on it with joy...

Instruction will come out of Zion, God's word from Jerusalem.

God will judge nations and bring justice to peoples,

And they shall beat their swords into plows,

And their spears into hooks for pruning trees:

Nation shall not take up sword against nation;

They shall never again know war.

[Source: Isaiah 2:2-4]

The Dead Sea Scrolls were wrapped in linen and hidden in caves in these pottery jars.

WORD SEARCH

Look across and down to find 10 hidden words. Use the words to complete the sentences.

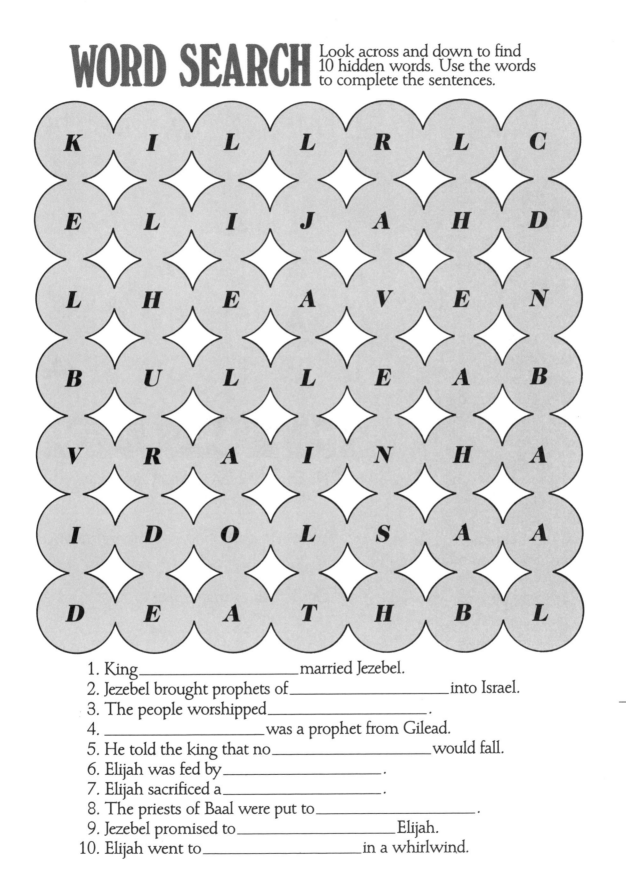

K	I	L	L	R	L	C
E	L	I	J	A	H	D
L	H	E	A	V	E	N
B	U	L	L	E	A	B
V	R	A	I	N	H	A
I	D	O	L	S	A	A
D	E	A	T	H	B	L

1. King_____married Jezebel.
2. Jezebel brought prophets of_____into Israel.
3. The people worshipped_____.
4. _____was a prophet from Gilead.
5. He told the king that no_____would fall.
6. Elijah was fed by_____.
7. Elijah sacrificed a_____.
8. The priests of Baal were put to_____.
9. Jezebel promised to_____Elijah.
10. Elijah went to_____in a whirlwind.

NAME S

Six **A**s are in the right place, but the other letters are all

```
B   R   A   A   A   M   H   A
I   E   L   H   A   J
S   I   A   C   A
A   A   B   H
J   A   O   B   C
L   E   H   S   I   A
```

WHAT HAPPENED WHEN?

1. What happened when King Ahab married Jezebel?
2. What happened when Elijah hid near Wadi Kerit?
3. What happened when Elijah met the priests of Baal on Mount Carmel?
4. What happened when Elijah was taken away?
5. What happened when Elisha struck the water with Elijah's robe?

WHO SAID IT TO WHOM?

1. "No rain shall fall unless I say it can,"

   said_____to_____.

2. "You must obey God's commandments,"

   said_____to_____.

3. "Cry louder. Perhaps Baal is busy,"

   said_____to_____.

4. "I will follow you,"

   said_____to_____.

5. "Do you know that God will take your master from you today?"

   said_____to_____.

6. "Nation shall not take up sword against nation,"

   said_____to_____.

CRAMBLE

mixed up. Write the names by putting the letters in the correct order.

__ __ __ **A** __ __ __

__ __ __ __ **A** __

__ __ **A** __ __

A __ __ __

__ __ **A** __ __ __

__ __ __ __ __ **A**

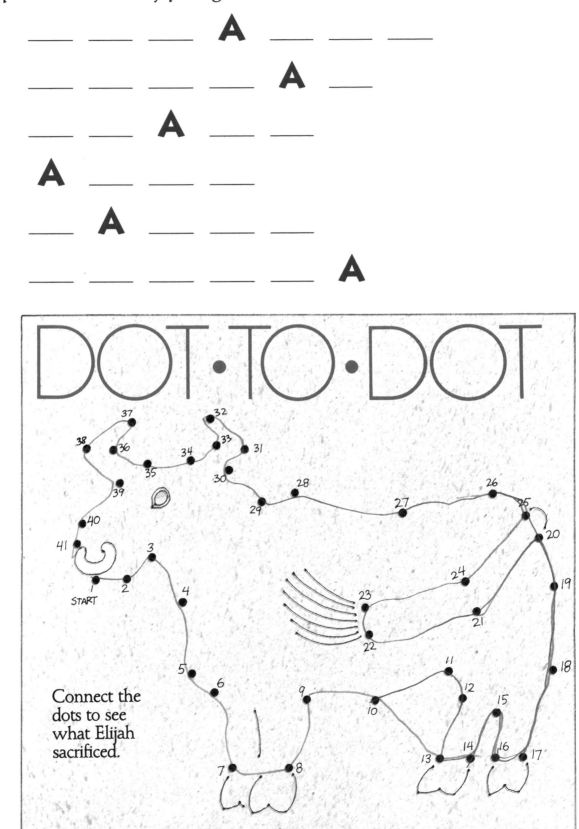

DOT·TO·DOT

Connect the dots to see what Elijah sacrificed.

Chapter 13

JONAH

od said to Jonah, "Leave Israel at once and go to Nineveh, that great city. Tell them that they will be destroyed, for I know the evil they have done."

Instead, Jonah tried to run away from God. He found a ship headed for Tarshish. He paid his fare and went aboard, to sail away from God.

God sent a great wind and a mighty storm on the sea. The ship tossed on the waves. It was near to breaking up. The sailors were afraid and every man prayed to his god. They even threw the cargo into the sea to make the ship lighter.

Jonah was fast asleep inside the ship. When the captain saw him, he shouted, "How can you sleep? Get up and pray to your God. Perhaps your God will save us!"

The men said, "Let us cast lots to see who has brought this trouble upon us." So they cast lots, and the lot fell on Jonah. Then Jonah said, "I am a Hebrew. And I have tried to run from the God of heaven, who made both sea and land."

"What must we do to you to make the sea calm?" they asked. And he said, "Throw me into the sea and it will be calm. This great storm is because of me." So they threw Jonah into the sea. And the storm ended and the sea grew still.

God sent a great fish that swallowed Jonah. Jonah was in the fish's belly three days and three nights. At last, Jonah prayed to God. And God commanded the fish to vomit Jonah onto dry land.

Again God said to Jonah, "Go at once to Nineveh, that great city. Deliver My message." And, this time, Jonah went to Nineveh.

Nineveh was enormous – it took three days to walk from one end to the other. Jonah entered the city and walked one full day, crying out, "In forty days Nineveh shall be destroyed!"

The people of Nineveh heard Jonah's words and believed God. They fasted. They took off their comfortable clothes and dressed in sackcloth. Even the king of Nineveh rose from his throne, took off his robe, covered himself with sackcloth, and sat in ashes.

God saw that the people were truly sorry. And God decided not to destroy the city of Nineveh after all.

All of this made Jonah unhappy. He even grew angry. "O God," he prayed, "I knew You would do this to me! You are a gentle God, slow to anger and filled with loving kindness. I knew that You would forgive this city. Now, O God, please take my life. I would rather die than live!"

God said, "Is it right for you to be so angry?"

Jonah left the city and went eastward. There he built a *sukkah* and sat in its shade. He sat and watched the city. God sent a plant to grow up over Jonah. And it shaded his head from the heat. So Jonah was very grateful for the plant.

When the sun rose, God brought a worm to attack the plant. The plant shriveled. And God brought an angry wind from the east. The sun beat down on Jonah's head, so that Jonah fainted. Then Jonah begged for death, saying, "I would rather die than live."

God said to Jonah, "Is it right for you to be so angry about the plant?" "Yes!" said Jonah, "I am so angry that I want to die!"

God said, "See now: You care that much for a plant which grew in a night and shriveled in a night. Should I not care for Nineveh, that great city, in which are more than one hundred and twenty thousand people? Though the people there are not wise, I care for them and also for their cattle."

Nineveh was the capital of the Assyrian Empire, a city filled with great palaces. One carving from a palace wall shows the king seated on his throne.

Jonah tried to run away from God.

Did Jonah really think that he could run away from God? Our sages say: this happened in the days when many believed that God lived in the Temple in Jerusalem. Jonah thought that he could escape God by leaving Israel. But the great teaching of the Book of Jonah is that the One God is not just the God of Israel but the God of all the earth. Our God is everywhere. In the Book of Jonah, God sends a Jewish prophet to the Assyrian city of Nineveh. Even more, the people of Nineveh accept God's words and repent. And, even more, God forgives them.

On a ship like this one, Jonah set sail to escape God. When the storm nearly destroyed the ship, the sailors threw Jonah overboard.

The Parable of Jonah

A parable is a short, simple story which is used to teach a lesson. Some teachers say that part of the Book of Jonah is a parable. Jonah is the Jewish people. God calls on the Jews to teach the commandments to all nations, just as Jonah was sent to Nineveh. Jonah is thrown into the sea, just as our people were sent out of Israel after the Second Temple was destroyed. Jonah lives in the belly of the fish just as our people live in foreign lands. And Jonah is returned to Israel by the fish, reminding us of God's promise to return all Jews back to the Promised Land.

If this is a parable, it does teach us a lesson: Even when Jonah is returned to Israel by the fish, God still wants him to go to Nineveh. In the same way, God still wants us to be a people of prophets—to teach God's commandments to all nations.

A gourd. Scholars believe that this was the plant which grew up to shade Jonah's head.

112

A Roman carving shows a sailing ship battling a storm on the Mediterranean Sea. It is easy to imagine how terrified the sailors must have been.

A LESSON FROM THE PROPHETS

Amos and Micah

The prophets Amos and Micah lived about the same time as Jonah and Isaiah. Amos taught that God loves justice more than sacrifices. Micah taught that God loves the rich and poor alike, and the rich must help the poor. Both of them agreed with the message of the Book of Jonah: The God of Israel is also the God of all the world.

From the book of the prophet Amos:

[God says:] I hate, I despise your festivals,
　I do not like your holy days.
You offer me sacrifices of animals and grain,

I do not accept them...
Do not sing Me your songs, or play Me your melodies.
　But let justice rush up like water,
And make righteousness a mighty stream.

From the book of the prophet Micah:

[Israel says:] What shall I bring when I come to God,
　When I bow before the Most High?
Shall I bring God sacrifices?...
　Will God be pleased with thousands of rams,
　With ten thousands of rivers of oil?...
[The prophet answers:] It has been told to you, O human, What is good and what God demands of you:
　Only to do justly,
　And to love mercy,
　And to walk humbly with your God.

[Sources: Amos 5:21-24; Micah 6:6-8]

Animal sacrifices were offered on altars like the one from the ruins of the city of Megiddo. At each corner, the altar had a "horn" or handle to hold the sacrifice in place while it burned. Amos and Micah taught that God does not really care about animal sacrifices. What does God really want?

113

Help Jonah find the way to Nineveh.

MAZE

WHAT IS TRUE?

Put a "T" beside each true statement. Put an "F" beside each statement that is not true.

- [ ] 1. The sailors were never worried because they were very brave.
- [ ] 2. God sent a great fish to swallow Jonah.
- [ ] 3. The people of Nineveh laughed at Jonah and called him crazy.
- [ ] 4. The king of Nineveh sat in ashes.
- [ ] 5. When God saved Nineveh, Jonah was very hungry.
- [ ] 6. God asked Jonah, "Why are you so angry?"
- [ ] 7. Jonah was angry because the plant was destroyed.
- [ ] 8. God saved the people of Nineveh.

114

SECRET WORDS

Unscramble the letters to see the words.

uSjLYt EMcyR uMbhLy

What does God want of you? To do _ _ _ _ _ _ _, and to love _ _ _ _ _ _, and to walk _ _ _ _ _ _ _.

THE REASONS WHY? Answer in your own words.

1. Why did Jonah try to run away from God?_____

_____

2. Why did the sailors throw Jonah into the sea?_____

_____

3. Why did God send a great fish to swallow Jonah?_____

_____

4. Why did God decide not to destroy the city of Nineveh?_____

_____

5. Why did God bring a worm to kill the plant?_____

_____

JIGSAW PUZZLE

DECIDED
LAND
CITY
SORRY
DESTROYED
FISH
SHIP
PRAYED
CALM
STORM

God told Jonah to go to the_____ of Nineveh. Instead, Jonah
went on a_____. God sent a mighty_____on the
sea. The sailors threw Jonah overboard and then the sea was_____.
A great_____swallowed Jonah. Jonah_____to God
and the fish threw Jonah onto dry_____. Jonah entered Nineveh
and warned the people that the city would be_____. The people
dressed in sackcloth and God saw that they were truly_____so
God_____not to destroy the city after all.

Chapter 14

JEREMIAH

n the days of the last three kings of Judah, Jeremiah was God's prophet. God said to Jeremiah, "Speak My words in the Temple. Perhaps the people will listen and stop doing evil. If so, I will forgive them and save them from destruction."

In the Temple, the priests and the prophets and all the people heard Jeremiah speak. And when Jeremiah was done, they grabbed him and would not let him go. "You will surely die!" they said. The princes of Judah came to the Temple. And the priests and prophets told them, "This man must die! He is a traitor to Jerusalem."

Jeremiah said, "God sent me to speak out against the Temple and against Jerusalem. Change your evil ways to good, and God may forgive you. As for me, my life is in your hands. Do what seems good and proper. But if you put me to death, you will have innocent blood on your hands."

The princes said, "This man does not deserve to die. He brings us a warning from God." And others said, "Micah brought us God's warning in days gone by, and he was not put to death! Truly, Micah's words saved us, because we stopped doing evil." Then Jeremiah was saved.

Another time, Jeremiah was hiding from the king. God said to Jeremiah, "Write down all the words I have spoken to you in a scroll."

117

Jeremiah asked Baruch to be his scribe. Baruch wrote down everything Jeremiah said, all the words of God. Jeremiah said, "I must hide. I cannot go to the Temple. You must go and read God's words from the scroll. Let the people hear. Perhaps they will change their ways." And Baruch went to the Temple to read aloud the words of the scroll.

The princes listened to Baruch. They took his scroll. "Go and hide with Jeremiah," they told him. "Let no one know where you are." Now when the king heard about the scroll, he called for it to be brought to him. It was winter, and there was a fire burning to warm the king. And when the king saw the scroll, he slashed it with a knife and threw it into the fire. He paid no attention to the words. And the people did not turn away from evil.

Baruch took another scroll and wrote again all the words that God had spoken to Jeremiah.

Again, God's word came to Jeremiah. He spoke out against the princes of Judah and they lowered Jeremiah into a deep well. King Zedekiah heard

that the prophet was dying in the well. He sent men with ropes to save Jeremiah.

Now Jeremiah the prophet was locked up in the king's prison. "Why do you tell us terrible things?" asked Zedekiah. "Why do you say that God will give Jerusalem to the king of Babylon? Why do you say: 'Zedekiah king of Judah shall not escape. He will be captured and taken to Babylon?' Why do you steal our hope, instead of giving us hope for victory?"

Jeremiah said, "I speak the truth. The city will be destroyed and the people will be taken captive. Yet, there is hope. God will remember the people of Israel. God will bring them back to Jerusalem. Then God will show them mercy and give us them this land forever. God will make Israel great, as of old."

Nebuchadnezzar, king of Babylon, and all his army camped around Jerusalem. They let no one in or out. After four months, the people of Jerusalem began to starve because there was no food in the city. Finally, the Babylonians broke through the walls of Jerusalem. The king and his soldiers ran away by night, but the Babylonians chased them. They trapped Zedekiah in the plains of Jericho. And they brought Zedekiah to Nebuchadnezzar. As Zedekiah watched, the king of Babylon killed his sons. He killed all the princes of Judah. Then he put out Zedekiah's eyes, took Zedekiah to Babylon, and put him in prison till the day of his death.

The Babylonians burned the Temple and all the great houses of Jerusalem. The army of Babylon destroyed the walls of Jerusalem. They took many people captive, leaving only the poor behind. They also took the pots, the shovels, the bowls, the spoons – all the bronze, silver, and gold that belonged to the Temple.

One generation passed. A new king arose in Babylon. He brought out the man who was king of Judah before Zedekiah. He spoke kindly to the old man, calling him king again. He gave the king of Judah an important seat among the many kings who lived in Babylon. So the words of Jeremiah came true. There was yet hope for the people of Israel.

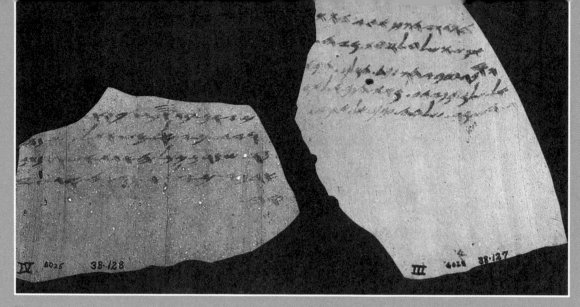

Two of "the Lachish letters." The writing is in an early kind of Hebrew lettering.

WHAT DOES IT MEAN?

"Why do you steal our hope...?"

Zedekiah did not want to hear the harsh words of Jeremiah. He wanted Jeremiah to tell him that God would save Jerusalem, and save Zedekiah. He said that Jeremiah's words were stealing hope from the people.

Not long ago, archaeologists digging at Tel Lachish discovered "the Lachish letters." The "letters" are on pieces of broken pottery. They were written in the time of Jeremiah, when Lachish was a large city. They are reports from a guard post to the commander of the city. In one letter, the guard asks if the commander has read a scroll sent by "the king and the princes" of Jerusalem. The guard says, "Lo, the words of the princes are not good. They make us weak instead of making us strong. Truly, I have been worried, since I read these words..." The guard had good reason to worry. Soon after he wrote to the commander, the city of Lachish was destroyed by the Babylonians.

If the truth is not pretty, we do not want to hear it. We want the people who speak to us to tell us only good news. Some people do this. But not a prophet. As Jeremiah said to King Zedekiah, "I speak the truth."

A carving from Nineveh shows the soldiers of Babylon attacking the city of Lachish.

WHAT DOES IT TEACH?
The Last Days of Jeremiah

Nebuchadnezzar knew that Jeremiah was in the royal prison. He sent soldiers to set the prophet loose. Jeremiah went to a small town just north of Jerusalem. After a few months of peace, he had to run away again— this time from the Babylonians. He went to Egypt. He wrote letters to the Jews who had been taken as captives to Babylonia. All was not lost, he told them, if they put their trust in God. Then he spoke for God: "The people shall return from the enemy's land.…There is hope for your future. I will heal you and cure you of your wounds.…The city shall be rebuilt on its mound, and the fortress in its rightful place." Jeremiah died in Egypt. But his words gave real hope to the Jews in Babylonia, and Judaism did not die.

After the battle of Lachish, Jewish prisoners were taken to Babylon.

A LESSON FROM THE WRITINGS
The Book of Lamentations

Jeremiah was there when Jerusalem fell and the Temple was destroyed. Our sages say: In his last days, Jeremiah wrote the Book of Lamentations. It is a book of sad remembering. We read Lamentations each year on *Tisha Be'Av,* the day of fasting in memory of the Temple. Here are a few lines from Lamentations:

> How the city sits all alone, though once it was full of people!
> Now the city is like a widow.

> Surely God's mercy is not exhausted,
> God's compassion does not fail.
> They are new every morning…

> The crown is fallen from our head.
> Woe to us! For we have sinned…
> Now foxes walk on the bare mountain of Zion.

> Return us to You, O God, and we shall be returned,
> Renew our days of old.

[Source: Lamentations]

This monument tells of the victories of the Assyrian King Sennacherib. The smaller picture shows an impression made by the seal of a Hebrew scribe. Seals were used much the way we use signatures today.

121

THE CORRECT ANSWER

All these things happened, but they are not in the right order.
Number the sentences in the order that they happened.

_____Jeremiah hid from King Zedekiah.

_____The king of Babylon put out Zedekiah's eyes.

_____Jeremiah spoke in the Temple.

_____Baruch wrote Jeremiah's words on a scroll.

_____The princes of Judah put Jeremiah into a well.

_____The king burned Baruch's scroll.

_____The Babylonians burned the Temple.

MAKE THE CONNECTIONS

Each of these four kings was advised by a prophet. Unscramble each prophet's name.

KINGS	*PROPHETS*	*ANSWERS*							
ZEDEKIAH	EJMERAHI								
AHAB	LIHJEA								
DAVID	TNAHNA								
SAUL	MESALU								

OPPOSITES

Like the other prophets, Jeremiah taught the people right from wrong.
Each word in the first column means the opposite of a word in the second column.
Use lines to connect the opposites.

GOOD	HATE
MERCIFUL	EVIL
KIND	WRONG
JUST	PROUD
HUMBLE	UNFAIR
LOVE	CRUEL
RIGHT	HEARTLESS

You Be a Scribe

Baruch was Jeremiah's scribe.
He wrote everything
Jeremiah said on a scroll.
Choose some of Jeremiah's words
and write them here.

LOOKING FOR UNDERSTANDING

Circle the words that best complete each sentence.

1. Jeremiah spoke God's words in the Temple so that the people would not
   pray.   go to Babylonia.   do evil.

2. Baruch wrote everything Jeremiah said on
   pottery.   a scroll.   the walls of the Temple.

3. When King Zedekiah saw Baruch's scroll, he
   read it.   threw it into a well.   burned it.

4. When Zedekiah heard that Jeremiah was in a well, he
   let him die.   sent men to save him.   killed his sons.

5. When the Babylonian army camped around Jerusalem, the people
   began to starve.   celebrated Sukkot.   went to Egypt.

6. We read the Book of Lamentations on
   Yom Kippur.   Shabbat.   Tisha Be'Av.

123

THE BOOK OF JOB

nce upon a time in the land of Uz, there lived a man named Job. Job was a good man. He believed in God and hated evil. He had seven sons and three daughters. He owned sheep and camels, oxen and donkeys by the thousands. Job was the richest man in the East.

Then all the angels gathered before God, even Satan – the angel who argues against human beings. God said to Satan, "Have you seen My servant Job? He is a good man."

Satan answered, "You make it easy for Job to be good. You bless him and give him riches. But if you took away all you have given him, he would curse You soon enough!"

"I will let you test Job," God said. "You may take anything he has, but do not harm him."

A messenger came to Job and said, "The oxen and donkeys were in the field when raiders came and took them away. Indeed, the raiders killed all your servants. Only I escaped to tell you!" While the servant was still speaking, another messenger came. "Lightning fell from heaven," he said. "It burned your sheep and all your shepherds. Only I escaped to tell you!" And while the shepherd was still speaking, another also came and said, "Your camels have been stolen and their keepers killed. Only I escaped to tell you!"

While he was still speaking, another messenger came and said, "Your sons and daughters were gathered at the house of your oldest son. Suddenly, a whirlwind came and struck the house. All your children are dead!"

Then Job rose from his chair. He ripped his robe and began to pray. "I came into this world with nothing, and I will take nothing out when I die. God gave, and God has taken away. Blessed be God."

God said to Satan, "Have you seen My servant Job? You have taken away his family and his riches, and yet he still believes in Me!"

Satan answered, "People will believe in You as long as they do not suffer pain. But if You touch his bone and flesh, Job will curse You soon enough!"

So God said to Satan, "Go and test him. Only do not take Job's life."

Satan made Job ill so that his skin blistered in pain from the bottom of his foot to the top of his head. Job's wife said, "Do you still believe in God? You should curse God!" But Job answered, "Do not speak foolishness. We take our good times from God. We must take the bad times, as well."

Job had three good friends—Eliphaz, Bildad, and Zophar—and they came to comfort him. For seven days and seven nights, they sat beside him without saying a word.

At last, Job spoke. "I wish I had not been born." Then Eliphaz said, "Do not be angry. People should be happy when God punishes them for doing wrong. That is the truth!"

Job answered, "If my suffering was weighed on a scale, it would be heavier than the sand on the seashore. O God, what are human beings? Why do You make them great? What have I done to You? And why do You not forgive me?"

Bildad said, "Your words are empty like the wind. God is good. Your children sinned, and God punished them with death. If you were really good, God would answer your prayers. God would make you rich again."

Job answered, "How can any person be good in God's eyes? All of us do some evil–no person is perfect. I just want God to tell me what I have done wrong."

Then Zophar said, "If God gave you wisdom you would know that you are being punished even *less* than you deserve! Pray to God with all your heart. Then God will make your life brighter than the sun at noon."

Job answered, "Do you really think that your wisdom is greater than mine? Silence should be your wisdom! Why do you tell lies about me and say they come from God? I love God with all my heart. Even though God kills me, yet I trust God. In the end, God will judge me and see that I am good."

Then Eliphaz spoke again. "Evil speaks through your mouth. You talk with a sly tongue, but your prayers do not come from your heart."

Job answered, "You three bring me no comfort! If you were in my place, I could talk as you do. But I would not! I would try to make you feel better."

Bildad spoke again. "Why be angry at us? You are the one who suffers for doing wrong. Should God change the world for you? Not for one who is wicked!"

Job answered, "No. I have not done wrong to God. God has done wrong to me. I cry aloud, but there is no justice. Pity me, my friends, for

God punishes me for no reason."

Zophar spoke again. "The wicked must suffer. Their hour of glory is short. Suffering is what God gives the wicked."

Job answered, "Listen to me: There is a mine for silver, and a place for making gold pure. But where can wisdom be found? Wisdom is not found in the land of the living. I cry out to God, but God does not answer me. God has turned against me!"

So the three men stopped answering Job. But a young man named Elihu was there. Elihu was angry because Job called God unjust. Elihu said to Job, "Great men are not always wise. Old ones do not always understand justice. You say that you have not been wicked, but that is a wicked answer! God is greater than we! God is always speaking to us, yet we do not always listen. God's wonders are all around us. Can you look into the sun and not be blinded? God's justice is always straight!"

Then God answered Job out of the whirlwind. "Why do you speak without knowing? Get ready, for I will question you. Where were you when I created the earth? Do you tell the eagle when to fly? Should you correct God? Do you question My judgment? Do you have God's strength? Can you thunder with God's voice?"

Job said to God, "I know that You can do everything. You speak of things too wonderful for me. Yet, before, only my ear had heard of You, but now my eyes see You. I tell You now: I am nothing. And I pray to You: Forgive me."

After God spoke these words to Job, God said to Eliphaz, "I am angry at you and your two friends. My servant Job spoke fairly, and you did not." Then the three friends prayed for God's forgiveness. And Job also prayed for them. So God gave Job twice as much as he had before.

God blessed Job with sheep and camels, oxen and donkeys. God gave him seven sons and three daughters. And Job lived one hundred and forty years, and saw his children and grandchildren for four generations. Then Job died, old and full of days.

The pictures in this book show Job's second family and the riches which God returned to Job after his great test.

WHAT DOES IT TEACH?
Satan and the Jews

Angels usually are not called by name in the Bible. But in this story one angel is called *hasatan,* "the Satan." Some sages say: Satan is the same as the Angel of Death. Most sages, however, agree that Satan is just another name for the *yetzer hara,* the voice in all of us that argues for us to do bad things. We also have another voice, the *yetzer tov,* that argues for us to do what is good. Christians often say that Satan is the devil, the enemy of God. But Jews do not believe in a devil.

WHAT DOES IT MEAN?
Once upon a time...

Was there ever a real man named Job? Our teachers argued about this question. Some said, Job lived in the time of Moses, and Moses wrote the Book of Job. Others said, Job lived while the Children of Israel were in Egypt. Still others said, Job lived in the times of Abraham, Nebuchadnezzar, Queen Esther, Solomon, or the Judges. One teacher said there was never any real Job, the whole book is a work of the imagination. But most of our teachers agree that the beginning of the story, the meetings between God and the angels is not real, even if Job was real. For this reason, the story begins, "Once upon a time..."

When we create and build, we follow the *yetzer tov* which teaches us to create just as God creates. What are some other ways we follow the *yetzer tov*?

Just as Ezekiel foretold, the bones of the House of Israel could come to life again. In our own time, the State of Israel is one way God has kept the promise to rebuild our people.

A LESSON FROM THE PROPHETS

Ezekiel and the Dry Bones

The Book of Job was a comfort to the Jews who had been taken away to exile in Babylonia. God tested Job with suffering, but finally everything was given back to Job. The prophet Ezekiel said that everything would be returned to the Jewish people, too. Here is Ezekiel's vision:

God set me in a valley full of dry bones. God said, "Can these bones live again?" I said, "O God, only You know." Then God told me to speak to the bones and say, "O dry bones! God will breathe life into you. God will put muscle on you and cover you with skin. God will make you live again. And you will know the One God!"

I spoke to the bones. Suddenly, there was a rattling sound and the bones came together. I looked, and muscle and skin were on them. Then the breath of life came from all sides and the bones stood up. They came to life in all their vast numbers.

God said, "These bones are the House of Israel. They say, 'Our hope is gone. Our bones are dried up.' But tell them, 'God will bring you out from the grave. God will put new life in you and you will live again,' "

[Source: Ezekiel 37:1-14]

130

WHO SAID IT?

A MESSENGER

BILDAD

JOB'S WIFE

ELIHU

JOB

EZEKIEL

ELIPHAZ

ZOPHAR

1. "O dry bones! God will breathe life into you," said_____.

2. "All your children are dead," said_____.

3. "Do you still believe in God?" said_____.

4. "People should be happy when God punishes them for doing wrong," said_____.

5. "If you were really good, God would answer your prayers," said_____.

6. "You are being punished even less than you deserve," said_____.

7. "God's justice is always straight," said_____.

8. "I am nothing. Forgive me," said_____.

131

Draw a Picture

God's wonders are all around us.
Draw something that is wonderful to you.

Think About It

Have you ever been accused of doing something you did not do? Have you ever been punished unfairly? How did you feel? What did you do?

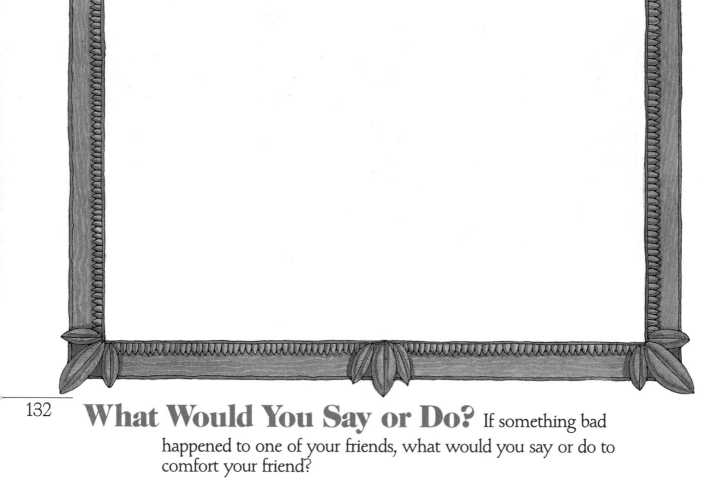

What Would You Say or Do? If something bad happened to one of your friends, what would you say or do to comfort your friend?

Hidden Message

Circle every other letter to see what God said to Job.

T	W	L	H	A	E	P	R	T	E	M
W	B	E	N	R	B	E	D	Y	G	O
J	U	V	W	X	H	F	E	B	N	C
I	O	C	Y	R	P	E	Q	A	S	T
K	E	G	D	L	T	A	H	D	E	M
E	P	A	N	R	O	T	R	H		

Write the message here: _____

_____

_____

Chapter 16

THE SCROLL OF ESTHER

hasuerus was the king of Persia. He made a feast in Shushan for all his followers. On the seventh day of the feast, when the king was merry with wine, he called for Queen Vashti, so that he could show off her beauty. Queen Vashti refused to come. The king was so angry that he sent Vashti away forever.

The king's servants said, "Let all the beautiful girls in the kingdom be brought to Shushan. The one the king likes best, shall be queen instead of Vashti." And it was done.

There was a Jew in Shushan named Mordecai. Mordecai treated his cousin Esther as his daughter, for she was an orphan. Now Esther was beautiful and she was taken to the palace, to see if she would be queen. The king loved Esther more than all the other women. He set the royal crown on her head and made her queen. But Esther did not tell anyone that she was Jewish.

Every day, Mordecai sat in the king's gate. Now it happened that he heard two of the king's servants planning to kill King Ahasuerus. Mordecai told Esther, and Esther told the king what Mordecai had said. The two evil servants were hanged, and a report was written in the chronicles of the king.

After these things, King Ahasuerus appointed an evil man named Haman to be his chief minister. All the king's servants bowed to Haman, as the king commanded, but Mordecai would not bow down. When Haman saw that Mordecai the Jew would not bow down, he grew angry. Haman decided to destroy Mordecai and all the Jews of Persia. Haman asked the priests to choose the best date and they cast *Pur* ("the lot"). So the date was set in the month of Adar.

Haman said to King Ahasuerus, "There is a certain people scattered in all the cities of your kingdom. They do not follow the king's laws. Let the king send out an order to destroy them."

The king handed his signet ring to Haman. "The people and their money are yours," said the king. "Do whatever you please."

When Mordecai heard that the Jews had fallen into Haman's evil hands, he cried out. He would not be comforted. Jews everywhere fasted, wept, and mourned. Esther heard, and she too was upset. Mordecai sent

a message to Esther, saying, "Go to the king. Plead for the life of our people!"

But Esther sent a message to Mordecai, saying, "I cannot visit the king. Any person who visits the king without being called is put to death—unless the king holds out his golden scepter."

Mordecai answered Esther. "Do not think that you will escape when all other Jews are put to death. If you are silent now, the Jews will still be saved somehow. Yet, who knows: Perhaps you were made queen so that you might save our people!"

Esther told Mordecai: "Gather all the Jews in Shushan. Fast for three days. Then I will go to the king, though it is against the law. And if I perish, I perish!" Mordecai did as Esther asked.

On the third day, Esther put on her finest robes and went to the king's throne room. And the king was glad to see her! He held out his golden scepter and called Esther near. "Ask whatever you want," said the king. And Esther said, "I come to invite you and Haman to a feast."

When Haman heard, he was joyful that the queen had invited him. He could hardly wait for the day of the feast. But when he passed Mordecai in the king's gate, Mordecai still did not bow before him. And Haman was again filled with anger.

That night the king could not sleep. His servants brought the chronicles and read them to the king. That is how the king remembered that Mordecai had saved his life. The king asked, "What reward has Mordecai received for this?" And his servants answered, "None."

The king commanded, "Bring Haman to me." Then the king asked Haman, "What shall be done for the man the king wishes to honor?" And Haman imagined that the king wanted to honor him. Haman said, "To honor the man, let him wear one of the king's robes and let him ride one of the king's horses. Then let him parade on horseback through the city. And announce before him, 'This is the man the king wishes to honor!'"

Then the king said to Haman, "Take the robe and the horse, as you have said, and make a parade for Mordecai the Jew." And Haman was forced to do all this.

At last, the king and Haman went to dine with Queen Esther.

On the second day of the banquet, the king again said to Esther, "Ask whatever you want, Queen Esther. Ask and your wish shall be granted."

Then Queen Esther said, "If it pleases the king, I ask only for my life and the life of my people. For there is one who tries to destroy us!"

King Ahasuerus asked, "Who is this destroyer, and where is he?"

Esther said, "Our enemy is this wicked Haman!" And Haman was terrified before the king and queen. Haman begged Esther to save him. But a servant of the king said, "Look! You can see the gallows which Haman built for Mordecai." Then the king said, "Hang Haman on the gallows instead!" So they hanged evil Haman.

Afterward, King Ahasuerus called Queen Esther and Mordecai. They dressed Mordecai in clothes of blue and white and royal purple, and they put a crown of gold on his head.

The Jews had light and gladness, joy and honor, a feast and a holiday. Many of the people of the land became Jews. Mordecai wrote everything down, sending letters to Jews everywhere, telling them to celebrate *Purim* every year. For on the fourteenth day of the month of Adar, we were saved from our enemies.

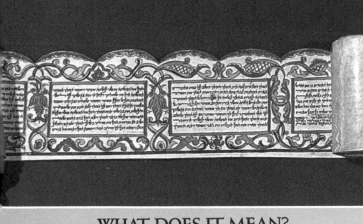

The *Megillah*, the Scroll of Esther, is often copied out by scribes as a separate book, and is sometimes beautifully decorated like this one.

This tomb in Persia (modern Iran) is called the tomb of Mordecai and Esther.

WHAT DOES IT MEAN?

There was a Jew in Shushan...

This is the first time that the Bible uses the word *Jew.* Before this the Bible calls us Hebrews, Children of Israel, People of Israel, and Israelites. The Hebrew word for Jew is *yehudi,* and it comes from the word *yehudah,* "Judah." At first, a Jew was any Hebrew who came from the southern kingdom of Judah. But the word came to mean anyone who was a member of the Children of Israel.

When we lived among people of other religions, our religion needed a name, too. Since it was the religion of the Jews, it was called *Judaism.* Today, we still call ourselves *Jews,* and we still call our religion *Judaism.*

WHAT DOES IT TEACH?

The Feasts of Persia

The story of Esther takes place in the royal court of Persia. King Ahasuerus is probably Xerxes I (485-464 B.C.E.).

His capital city was the huge city of Susa. Shushan was the name of his winter palace.

The Persians were known for their great feasts. The feast given by Ahasuerus at the beginning of this story lasted one hundred and eighty days! Probably the guests came and went, but the king went right on celebrating. Perhaps Vashti was tired of being called, over and over and over again, to appear at this endless feast and that is why she refused to come.

A Jewish painting from a third-century synagogue wall shows Haman leading Mordecai's horse in a parade through Shushan.

The Book of Chronicles

The chronicle of Ahasuerus was like a royal diary. The Bible has two books of Chronicles. Our Chronicles tell the whole history of the Children of Israel. Here, from Chronicles, is a story of King Solomon, David's wise son. As you read it, you will see a great difference between Solomon and Ahasuerus.

> The queen of Sheba heard of Solomon's wisdom and came to Jerusalem to test him. She brought camels loaded with spices, gold, and precious stones. She tried Solomon with riddles and questions, but Solomon answered every one. There was nothing that Solomon did not know. She said, "Everything I heard about you is true. It is because God loves Israel that God made you king to rule in justice!" The queen of Sheba gave Solomon many gifts.
>
> And he gave her gifts, too, anything she wanted. Then she and her servants returned to her land.

Can you see how Solomon and Ahasuerus differed? Ahasuerus loved feasts. Solomon loved learning.

[Source: II Chronicles 9:1-12]

140

Solomon's Pillars. Near these mighty rock columns in southern Israel, archaeologists discovered copper mines used in the time of King Solomon. Legend says that Solomon also had gold mines, but all we have found so far are these mines for copper. Whether or not he had gold mines, Solomon was the richest of all the Jewish kings.

Write Your Own Purim Megillah

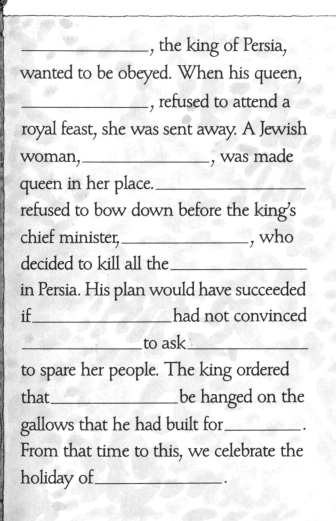

_____, the king of Persia, wanted to be obeyed. When his queen, _____, refused to attend a royal feast, she was sent away. A Jewish woman, _____, was made queen in her place. _____ refused to bow down before the king's chief minister, _____, who decided to kill all the _____ in Persia. His plan would have succeeded if _____ had not convinced _____ to ask _____ to spare her people. The king ordered that _____ be hanged on the gallows that he had built for _____. From that time to this, we celebrate the holiday of _____.

BE A DECTECTIVE

How do you know that...
- Esther was unsure of herself.
- Ahasuerus was not a strong ruler.
- Mordecai was a good Jew.
- Haman loved power.

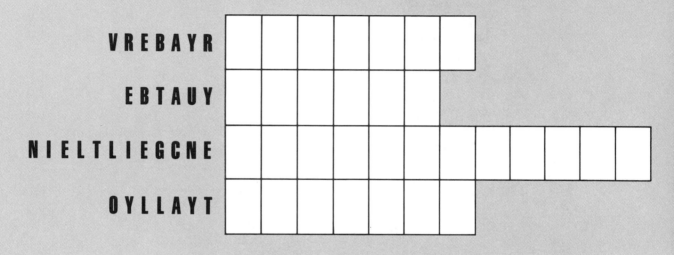

Unscramble each word to see four things that made Esther special.

VREBAYR

EBTAUY

NIELTLIEGCNE

OYLLAYT

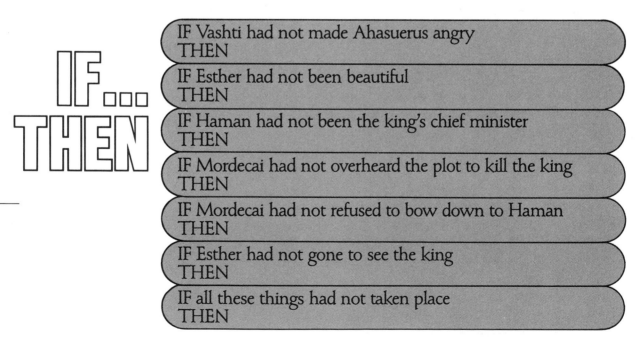

IF Vashti had not made Ahasuerus angry
THEN

IF Esther had not been beautiful
THEN

IF Haman had not been the king's chief minister
THEN

IF Mordecai had not overheard the plot to kill the king
THEN

IF Mordecai had not refused to bow down to Haman
THEN

IF Esther had not gone to see the king
THEN

IF all these things had not taken place
THEN

IF... THEN

MAKE A MASK

On the holiday of *Purim* we dress in costumes and wear masks. Who will you be?
Esther, Mordecai, Haman, or Ahasuerus? Use the space below
to practice drawing your own Purim mask.

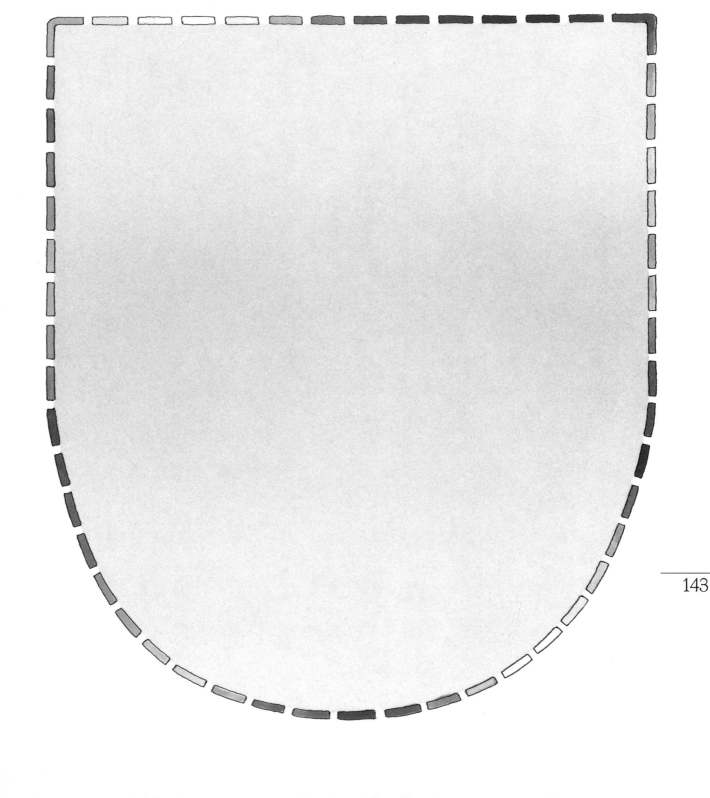

Daniel 1-3 דָּנִיֵּאל

Chapter 17

THE BOOK OF DANIEL

he king of Babylon opened a school for some of the young men of Judah, so that they could learn to serve the king. Daniel, Shadrach, Mishach, and Abednego were four of these young men. When their schooling was ended, they came before King Nebuchadnezzar. And these four were chosen from all the rest to serve the king. He liked them much better than all the magicians and fortune tellers in his kingdom.

One night, Nebuchadnezzar had a dream that troubled him so that he could not sleep. The king called all his magicians to tell him what he had dreamed. But they said, "No one, except the king, can tell what the king dreamed. No king has ever asked such a thing!" Then the king was furious. He ordered that all the wise men of Babylon should be killed.

They began killing the wise men. They looked for Daniel and his friends, to kill them. But Daniel came to the king and asked for a little time, so that he might be able to explain what the king had dreamed. Then Daniel went home and asked his three friends to pray for help.

When Daniel was asleep, the secret came to him in a dream. Then Daniel blessed God.

The king said to Daniel, "Can you tell me my dream and what it means?" Daniel answered, "No wise man or magician can tell it. But God knows every secret. Your dream came from God to tell you the future." And Daniel explained the dream. Then Nebuchadnezzar bowed down to Daniel. "Your God is truly the God of kings," said the king.

Nebuchadnezzar made Daniel ruler over Babylon, and chief over all the wise men of Babylon. And Shadrach, Mishach, and Abednego served Daniel in Babylon.

Once Nebuchadnezzar made a statue of gold and placed it in Babylon. Then the king's order was cried aloud. "To all peoples, nations, and languages: You shall bow down to worship this golden image. Whoever does not bow down to worship shall be thrown into a blazing furnace." All the people bowed down to worship the statue.

At that time, some jealous magicians came to Nebuchadnezzar and said, "O king, you said that anyone who does not worship the golden image will be thrown into a blazing furnace. We have seen three Jews who would not bow down – Shadrach, Mishach, and Abednego."

Nebuchadnezzar was filled with rage. They brought the three Jews before him. "Is it true that you do not bow to my gods?" he asked them. But the three would not worship the idol. So Nebuchadnezzar commanded his servants to heat the furnace seven times hotter than usual. Then Shadrach, Mishach, and Abednego were bound with rope and thrown into the blazing furnace. The fires were so hot that the men who threw the three friends into the furnace were burned alive.

Suddenly, King Nebuchadnezzar stood up in amazement. "Look!" the king said. "There are four men walking in the flames. And they are alive! The fourth one looks like an angel!" Nebuchadnezzar went near the mouth of the furnace. And Shadrach, Mishach, and Abednego came out of the flames. The fire had not burned them or their clothing. Not one hair on their head was singed.

Nebuchadnezzar said, "Blessed be the God of Shadrach, Mishach, and Abednego. For God sent an angel to save them. Now I order that any one who speaks against the God of Israel shall be put to death!" And the king did great honor to the three friends.

After Nebuchadnezzar, Daniel served King Darius. But the other magicians were still jealous. They said to the king, "Make an order that no one should pray to any god but you." And when the order was signed and sealed, they came to Daniel, while Daniel was praying to God. "The punishment is in the king's order," they said. "You will be thrown into a den of lions." They brought him to Darius, and Darius was sad because he liked Daniel. But Darius could not save Daniel, for he had sealed his order. And Daniel was thrown into the lions' den, and a great rock was rolled up to seal the entrance.

All night long the king fasted and did not sleep. The moment the sun rose, he rushed to the den of the lions, shouting out, "Daniel, O Daniel, did your God save you from the lions?" And the voice of Daniel came from behind the rock. "O my king, live forever. My God sent an angel who closed the mouths of the lions." Then Daniel was taken from the lions' den. And the king sent for the magicians who had tricked him. And he threw them into the den of lions. They barely reached the ground before the lions began to tear at them and crush their bones.

Then Darius sent an order through all the kingdom, saying, "All people shall tremble before the God of Daniel, the Living God. For God saves the righteous, as God saved Daniel from the power of the lions!"

The court of the Babylonian king shown on a wall carving. Daniel served as an adviser to the king.

WHAT DOES IT MEAN?

...While Daniel was praying to God.

The Book of Daniel tells us about life in Babylonia. Daniel and his three Jewish friends kept the laws of *kashrut*—eating only *kosher* foods, even when they lived in the palace. People fasted when they felt that they were in danger. And Daniel faced Jerusalem and prayed three times a day. The Jews, living in a foreign land, made a difficult and important choice. They decided to live as Jews, to continue walking in God's ways. We have to keep making that choice every day, no matter where we live.

148

The Gate of Ishtar, entrance to the ancient city of Babylon. Babylon was one of the most beautiful cities of the ancient world.

WHAT DOES IT TEACH?

Daniel and Miracles

The story of Daniel is full of miracles. The book tells of Babylonia, where people loved to hear miracle stories. But the miracle stories in the Book of Daniel teach about the might and power of God. God sends angels to rescue people from flaming furnaces and dens of lions. Then the kings learn that the God of the Jews is all-powerful. So, the real reason for telling these stories was to show that the One God rules over even the kings of Babylonia and Persia.

A LESSON FROM THE PROPHETS

The Second Isaiah

The Book of Isaiah is actually two books, the words of two different prophets. We have already met the first Isaiah in Chapter Twelve. We don't know the name of the other prophet. His book was added to the end of the Book of Isaiah, so we call him Second Isaiah. Here are words he spoke to the Jews in Babylon:

> Comfort, O comfort My people, says your God.
> Speak gently to Jerusalem.
> Tell her:
>> Her years of slavery are ended;
>> Her sin is forgiven.
> God has punished her twice for all her sins.

[Source: Isaiah 40: 1-2]

This place is said to be the burial site of Daniel. It is located in what was once Persia, near the city of Susa where Esther and Mordecai are also buried.

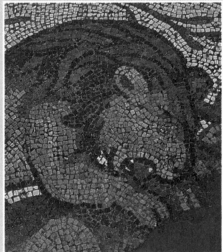

Mountain lions were common throughout the biblical world. Daniel was thrown into a den of hungry lions, but his faith in God saved him. This may not be a story about lions at all. It may have a hidden meaning. Can you guess what this story might really be telling us?

NAME SEARCH

Look across and down to find the names of 16 people you know.
Circle each name as you find it.

```
D  G  C  A  B  E  D  N  E  G  O  L  B  P
A  W  I  R  V  S  J  E  R  E  M  I  A  H
N  E  B  U  C  H  A  D  N  E  Z  Z  A  R
I  Z  J  I  S  A  I  A  H  O  J  O  B  N
E  H  O  D  A  D  Y  R  E  L  I  J  A  H
L  M  N  A  U  R  M  I  S  H  A  C  H  E
I  S  A  V  L  A  X  U  K  R  U  T  H  Q
U  D  H  I  J  C  P  S  E  S  T  H  E  R
A  T  M  D  N  H  E  Z  E  K  I  E  L  F
```

WHAT HAPPENED WHEN?

What happened
- when the magicians could not tell the king what he dreamed?
- when Daniel explained the king's dream?
- when the king ordered the people to worship the golden image?
- when the three friends were thrown into the blazing furnace?
- when Daniel was thrown into a den of lions?

WHAT DO YOU DREAM?

Have you had an interesting dream?
Use the space to draw it or write about it.

Making Choices

The story tells us about Jews who lived in a land outside Israel and continued to live as Jews. Name three Jewish things you do to walk in God's ways.

1 _____

2 _____

3 _____

WHAT IS TRUE?

Place a "T" beside each true sentence and an "F" beside each sentence which is not true.

- [ ] 1. Nebuchadnezzar did not like the four Jewish students in his school.
- [ ] 2. Nebuchadnezzar wanted his magicians to tell him what he dreamed.
- [ ] 3. As soon as the king asked, Daniel knew what the king had dreamed.
- [ ] 4. Nebuchadnezzar threw three men into the fire, but saw five men in it.
- [ ] 5. Daniel took food into the lion's den to feed the hungry lions.
- [ ] 6. Daniel took a thorn from a lion's paw so that all the lions liked him.
- [ ] 7. Darius liked Daniel very much and was glad when Daniel was saved.
- [ ] 8. Darius threw the magicians who had tricked him into the fiery furnace.
- [ ] 9. In Babylonia, the Jews decided to continue walking in God's ways.

REBUS

King Darius sent an order through all the kingdom saying:

All 🫛-ple shall trem-🐂 B·4 the God of Dan-🙂 4 God saves the righteous, as God saved Dan-🙂 from the 💥POW💥-er of the 🦁 s

EZRA AND NEHEMIAH

od stirred the spirit of Cyrus, the king of Persia, who ruled in Babylonia. Then Cyrus wrote this command and sent it to all his kingdom:

> Thus says Cyrus king of Persia: The heavenly God commands me to build a house of God in the land of Judah. Let the Jewish people of my kingdom go up to Jerusalem and build their Temple for the God of Israel!

God touched the hearts of many leaders of the tribes of Judah and Benjamin—and the priests and the Levites. Nearly 50,000 gathered to go. King Cyrus gave them everything that was taken from the First Temple. And the group returned to Jerusalem.

Seven months later, they started to work on the Second Temple. A large crowd of Jews gathered around them. Most people cheered, shouting and singing with joy. The older people, however, wept loudly because they could still remember the First Temple. That day, people could not tell the joy from the weeping.

Now, the pagans heard that the Jews were building a new Temple.

They said, "Let us help you." But the Jews said, "We must build it alone, as Cyrus the king commanded." Then the pagans became their enemies and did all they could to stop the Jews. So the work went slowly.

Then the prophets Haggai and Zechariah came. They lifted the hopes of the builders with God's words. And, at last, the Temple was finished—just as God commanded and the king of Persia ordered.

These are the words of Nehemiah, the adviser of the king of Persia: When I was serving the king in Shushan, Jewish messengers came from Judah. I asked, "Are things going well for the Jews and for Jerusalem?" And they said, "We need much help. The walls of Jerusalem are broken down and its wooden gates are burned."

I prayed, "O great God, open Your ear and hear my prayer. You promised that You would remember us and return us to our homeland. So let the king be kind to me. Let him send me to help my people in Jerusalem."

One day I was serving wine to the king. And he saw that I was sad—sadder than I had ever been before. "I know you are not ill," the king said to me. "This sadness must be in your heart."

I was filled with fear. I said, "O king, live forever! I am sad because my city is destroyed." The king asked, "What do you want to do?" I answered, "Please let me go up to Judah, to Jerusalem, to rebuild the city."

The king and queen asked me, "How long will you be gone?" And, in this way, the king gave me permission to go. He even sent army captains and horsemen to guard me along the way.

I came to Jerusalem and waited three days. That night, I rode secretly, all around the city. And everywhere I looked, the wall was in ruins.

Afterward, I said to the leaders of the Jewish people, "The walls of Jerusalem must be built again." And they said, "Then let us build!" When the pagans heard our plan, they laughed. "What are these weak Jews doing?" they asked. "Will they make walls from the burned stones, from the heaps of garbage?" But the Jewish people worked hard and soon we had built the wall half-way up and all around.

The pagans grew angry. They plotted to attack us. We prayed to God. And we set men to watch day and night, to warn us if the pagans came near.

The pagans said, "We will sneak up on the Jews and kill them." But we knew their plan.

I set men with swords, spears, and bows all along the lower parts of the wall. I spoke out, saying, "Do not be afraid of them. God will protect us."

From that time on, half of the workers built the wall, while the other half wore armor and carried weapons. With one hand the workers built, and in the other hand they also held weapons. Every builder had a sword. So the wall of Jerusalem was rebuilt and new gates were hung.

In the meanwhile, the king of Persia said to his servant Ezra, "Rise up and go to Jerusalem. Appoint judges over your people. And teach God's commandments to those who do not know them." Then Ezra the Scribe left Persia, taking many Jews with him to Jerusalem.

In the seventh month, all the people of Judah gathered together in Jerusalem. They told Ezra the Scribe to bring the Torah. Ezra stood on a wooden platform so that all could see him. And when he opened the scroll, all the people stood up. Ezra praised God. The people answered, "Amen, Amen!" And they bowed their heads and worshipped God. Then the leaders of the congregation read from the Torah, translating the Torah as they read, so that everyone could understand the words.

The next day, the leaders of the people came to study with Ezra the Scribe. And he taught them words of Torah. They heard God's commandment that the people should live in booths in the festival of the seventh month. Then they sent word to all the land of Judah, saying, "Prepare to celebrate the holiday of *Sukkot.*" They gave instructions for building booths, the *sukkot.* And, throughout the land, the people celebrated—it was the first time since the days of Joshua that the festival of *Sukkot* was celebrated in the land. Every day for seven days, Ezra taught them Torah and they celebrated. And on the eighth day the Jews gathered to offer great thanks to God.

Today, as we read the Torah in our synagogues, we often follow the example of Ezra the Scribe, explaining in English the meaning of the Hebrew.

WHAT DOES IT MEAN?

...translating the Torah as they read...

Our sages say: As the leaders read the Torah they translated it in two ways. First, many of the people had forgotten the Hebrew language. Instead, they spoke Aramaic. Hebrew and Aramaic are like English and German—they come from the same language family and share many words, but they are also different in many ways.

Second, the leaders had to explain the meaning of the words. When we read the scroll of the Torah, we are only reading "the written Torah." That is only one part of the teachings of Moses. The other part is "the spoken Torah," all the teachings which explain what the written Torah means.

WHAT DOES IT TEACH?

The Festival!

Today, we think of the High Holy Days—Rosh Hashanah and Yom Kippur—as our most important holi-days. But that was not true in the time of Joshua and from the time of Ezra onward. As long as the Jewish people lived in the Holy Land, the most important holiday was *Sukkot.* They called it *hehag,* "The Festival." On *Sukkot,* the farmers brought their harvest offerings to the Second Temple in Jerusalem. And Jerusalem was filled to overflowing—every street and every rooftop—with people living in booths for the seven days of *Sukkot.* We still remember that time today, as we build and decorate our *sukkot* and thank God for commanding us "to dwell in the *sukkah.*"

Decorating the *sukkah.* Do you know why we hang fruits and vegetables in honor of Sukkot?

Archaeologists discovered this cylinder which tells how Cyrus the Great conquered Babylon and allowed the Jews to return to Israel to rebuild the Temple.

Haggai and Zechariah

The Jews who returned to Jerusalem found life very difficult. The pagans were against them and did all they could to stop the building of the Temple. Just then two prophets appeared, Haggai and Zechariah. Haggai was older, and he remembered the beauty of the First Temple. Zechariah was younger, full of strong new promise.

From the words of Haggai:

[God says:] Why do you live in finished houses, and leave My house unfinished? Consider your ways! Be strong and work, for I am with you. And the glory of this second Temple shall be greater than the first. For in this place, I will bring peace.

From the words of Zechariah:

An angel of God came and woke me up, as if I was sleeping. The angel asked, "What do you see?" I said, "I see a golden menorah with seven branches. Two olive trees stand near it."

Then I asked, "What does it mean?" And the angel answered, "This is God's message: 'Not by might nor by power, but by My spirit [shall you win over your enemies]. Return to Me and I will return to you.'"

[Sources: Haggai 1:4-5; 2:4, 9; Zechariah 4:1-6]

This seven-branched menorah reminds us of the one which Zechariah saw in his vision. The seven-branched menorah is one of the most ancient symbols of the Jewish people and it is also used as the symbol of the modern State of Israel.

Choose the Best Word

1. David used his slingshot to [TICKLE] [KNOCK DOWN] [TRIP] Goliath.
2. Solomon used his wisdom to discover who was the [REAL] [BETTER] [SMARTEST] mother.
3. Elijah stopped [THE KING] [THE RAIN] [THE ARK OF THE COVENANT] from falling.
4. Jonah was angry and God made a [GOURD] [TENT] [PALM TREE] to shade him from the sun.
5. God answered Job out of the [PILLAR OF FIRE] [DRY BONES] [WHIRLWIND].
6. Mordecai treated Esther as a [WIFE] [DAUGHTER] [SERVANT].
7. Ezra taught [MATHEMATICS] [ARAMAIC] [TORAH] to the leaders of the people.
8. King Zedekiah heard that the prophet Jeremiah was [DYING] [HIDING] [PLAYING] in a deep well.
9. It took Solomon seven years to build [THE WALLS OF JERUSALEM] [THE TEMPLE] [THE ARK].
10. When God called, Samuel thought it was [MOSES] [HANNAH] [ELI THE PRIEST] calling him.

158

CHOOSE THE BEST

1. The prophets Haggai and Zechariah
   lifted the hopes of the builders of the Second Temple.
   told David that he should be punished.
   defeated the priests of Baal on Mount Carmel.
2. Joshua made the wall of Jericho fall down
   by kicking the bottom stones out.
   by circling the city seven times and blasting on the shofar.
   by shouting, "Open Sesame."
3. The Sea of Reeds split open and the Jews crossed on dry ground when
   Moses stretched out his hand over the sea.
   Gideon's men broke their pitchers and shouted.
   Miriam danced and sang.
4. Moses broke the two tablets of stone when
   he tripped on a rock on his way down the mountain.
   David shot him with a slingshot.
   he saw the people praying to the Golden Calf.
5. When she judged, Deborah
   sat beneath a palm tree in the land of Ephraim.
   was not a very good judge.
   stood near the Tabernacle at Shiloh.
6. Samson brought the house down when
   he leaned on the Ark of the Covenant.
   he felt Delilah cutting his hair.
   he pushed against the two columns holding up the Philistine temple.
7. Samuel told the people
   how a king would take away their children.
   that they should build a Temple for God.
   that three hundred soldiers would be enough.
8. Elijah was taken away by
   a field trip to Nineveh.
   a chariot of fire with horses of fire.
   the fourteenth day of the month of Adar.

MATCH THE STORIES

Use lines to connect the stories in the left column with the heroes in the column on the right.

S T O R Y

He came from Gilead and taught a lesson to the priests of Baal.

This judge led a battle and sang a song.

His three friends were no help at all when it came time to comfort him.

God sent this prophet out of Israel to speak to the people of Nineveh.

He had three friends who walked in flames.

This prophet's book in the Bible is really two books in one.

He was Moses' father-in-law, and he gave Moses good advice.

This judge chose three hundred men to help him defeat the Midianites.

She wanted to go wherever her Jewish mother-in-law would go.

He was the first king of Israel.

HERO

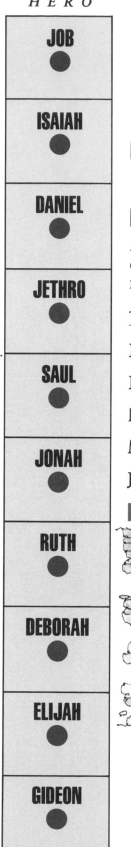

JOB

ISAIAH

DANIEL

JETHRO

SAUL

JONAH

RUTH

DEBORAH

ELIJAH

GIDEON

Teachers and Students

Match the teachers in the left column with their students in the right column.

TEACHERS	STUDENTS
ELIJAH	SAMUEL
ELI	MOSES
NATHAN	ELISHA
MOSES	DAVID
JETHRO	JOSHUA

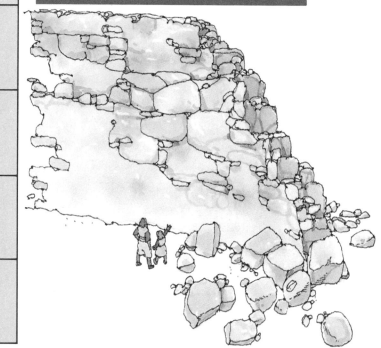

AFTERWORD

The Hebrew Bible tells the story of our people for more than one thousand five hundred years. Our sages taught: Moses said to the Jewish people, "God is ready to give us God's most treasured possession, the Torah. But God wants something in return—a surety, something that is precious to us. What shall we give to God as a surety?"

The people said, "Let us give God all the gold, rubies, and diamonds that we brought out of Egypt. They will be our surety." Moses said, "They are not enough. The light of the Torah is more brilliant than any diamond."

The people said, "Let us give God our great leaders—Moses and Aaron." Moses said, "It is not enough. Aaron and I already belong to God. We must give God something which is truly ours."

Then the people were lost in thought. What did they possess that was as precious as God's Torah?

At last, a wise old woman came forward to speak. "We have only one thing as precious as Torah," she said. "We must offer our children as a surety for the Torah. We will promise to teach the Torah faithfully to our children. Then they will promise to teach the Torah faithfully to their children. And, in this way, God will know that the precious Torah is in good hands."

Then Moses went up on Mount Sinai to receive the Torah. God gave the Torah to the world because the Jewish people pledged their children as a surety for the Torah.

From that time to this, we have taught the Torah to each new generation. And now your turn has come. Some day, you will have children of your own and you will want to teach them the lessons of the Torah, the words of the Prophets, and the teachings of the Writings.

The Bible ends with a new beginning—the building of the Second Temple. This book ends with a new beginning, too—it ends with you. For you are the new beginning of the Jewish people. What you do and what you think will become what the Jewish people does and what the Jewish people thinks. You are the surety. You are the pledge. May you live your life in the light of the Torah—as a blessing to your people and a blessing to your God.